TO CHOOSE THE FIRE
OF THE COSMOS

Using Our Soul Qualities to
Build a Better World

REBECCA A FIELD, Ph.D.

With a Foreword by the Dalai Lama

Love Your Life

Love Your Life Publishing

St. Peters, MO 63346

www.loveyourlifepublishing.com

ISBN: 978-1-934509-64-7

Library of Congress Control Number: 2012947499

Printed in the United States of America

First Printing 2012

Editing by Naomi Rose

Author Photo by Robin Ruth

Cover Art and Interior Design by Indie Designz

The author is grateful to the

Master Djwal Khul,

her master

teacher,

and his

amanuensis,

Alice A. Bailey,

who penned His

twenty-four volumes

used for the background of this work.

DEDICATION:

To the One of which/whom we are all a significant and important part,

the Hierarchy of Beings responsible for spiritual direction of humanity,

to the World Servers who are changing the face of the Earth for the better,

to my husband, Ken, for his constant spiritual support and wisdom

and to Naomi Rose for her encouragement and inspiration.

"He who realizes the sphere of space hidden in the cavern of his heart grasps all that may be desired and comes into contact with the Immensity."

—Taittiriya Upanisad

"To have a conscious realization of that Immensity is the desire that satisfies all desires."

—Michael Beckwith

"Someday, after we master the winds, the waves, the tides and gravity, we shall harness for God the energies of love, and for the second time in the history of the world, man will have discovered fire."

–Pierre Teilhard de Chardin

FOREWORD BY HIS HOLINESS THE DALAI LAMA

In this book, Dr. Rebecca Field highlights an important feature of life as a human being, the possibility of positive change. Because of this, all of us as individuals can play a valuable part in shaping the world around us by applying our consciousness and knowledge in joyful cooperation with others to create a more satisfactory order.

However, to create a great spiritual rebirth, we need to employ both the head and the heart. The Buddha always emphasized a balance of wisdom and compassion, which implies a sound brain and a good heart working together. Placing a greater importance on the intellect and ignoring the heart can cause increased problems and suffering in the world. On the other hand, if we totally neglect our intellectual capacity or our ability to think, then there is little difference between humans and animals. So, the two must be developed in harmony.

If the technological advances, we have now achieved, are to have beneficial consequence, there must be an accompanying inner development, a sense of responsibility for this small planet and the fellow inhabitants with whom we share it. It is time we discovered our human potential and the positive role that we can play in making this earth, our habitat, a place fit to live in. I am sure this book will contribute to creating such awareness.

His Holiness The Dalai Lama of TIBET

Table of Contents

WHAT IS "COSMIC FIRE"?

In "cosmic fire," there is a development of mind so that a fusion takes place within humankind, no differently than what happens in the cosmos or within an atom. When this happens, at this stage of development, heart and mind are not different. They are one, a perfect synthesis: mind/heart.

The time has come when we need to think in larger terms—on a cosmic level, as well as an earthly or personal level—and put our affairs and the current problems of the earth into a cosmic context. Only by doing this can we get the distance and objectivity needed to see and create our way into a positive future.

Mind/heart is an aspect of the soul, and indicates the quality of universality and inclusiveness. To understand this idea in human and cultural terms, think of Beethoven's 9th Symphony, which was an expression of his soul. He was totally deaf when he composed the music. He could not hear a note as he watched the symphony conducted for the first time in Vienna in 1824. Yet it was possibly the greatest piece of music ever written, eventually becoming the European Anthem. Is there a piece of classical music that better expresses the meaning of cosmic fire than Beethoven's 9th Symphony?

With this glorious music, Beethoven also opened a gate for light and love to penetrate and permeate the mindset of European nations and their peoples. It's as if he unconsciously created a tunnel in human consciousness through which the light of intelligent love could pass, in order for the modern European Union to come into existence. The power of the music itself created a subtle means for Europeans to create a political and economic union and end the belligerence behind long-term and innumerable wars. The European Union represents consciousness, or heart/mind tuned to the world of thought and meaning, the galaxy of universality, and the cosmos of inclusiveness. It is the powerful synthesis of the One. This is just one example of how "cosmic fire" can enter into human consciousness and affairs, and make a difference in our evolution towards the One.

Truth is within ourselves; it takes no rise
From outward things, whate'er you may believe.
There is an inmost center in us all
Where truth abides in fullness
. . . and to know
Rather consists in opening out a way
Whence the imprisoned splendor may escape
Than in effecting entry for a light
Supposed to be without.
    From *Paracelsus*

by Robert Browning

A NOTE TO THE READER

This is a book about evolutionary cosmology. But in case that sounds too distant from your own intimate life, too "out there," let me assure you that it's also about what's "in here"—in your own mind, heart, and soul. Surely, in our accelerating times, you have noticed around you, and perhaps also in your own life, that something seems to be moving forward in human experience, at the same time that other things are clearly breaking down. If we only focus on the breakdowns, real though they are, we miss the inspiration and the impetus for working in concert with our own highest potentials. For make no mistake: we are being called to evolve in the direction of our truest being, our soul, our oneness. We are being called, though we may or may not realize it; and we are being helped to evolve through subtle spiritual forces that have been with humanity for a very long time, but are closer to us now than ever before.

This book is about the cosmos inside the heart—extraordinarily beautiful, but not like the one in the sky. The fire in your heart and soul for a more meaningful, beautiful, good, and true life—both individually and culturally, throughout the world—

is not separate from the fire of the cosmos. It takes a different form, yet at the same time, humanity is—*you* are—essential to the fulfillment of our evolutionary promise.

This book is about the principle of wholeness. One of the most intriguing things about evolutionary cosmology is that life itself, in all its perfection and majesty, manifest and unmanifest, lies at the center of the cosmos. This book assumes that the cosmos is inside us as well as outside us. That's what people in our overly materialistic society are so hungry for—this life, this livingness. Infinitely precious, it is sought after more even than air. It has a magnetic, numinous attraction for humanity. When we can fully trust in the omnipresence and the omniscience of divine spirit, it will pull us through this most extremely difficult time in the history of humanity. It will help us build towards critical mass. There are stirrings in humanity that are unmistakable.

If you are holding this book in your hand, you are one of the people who has been called to serve this higher evolution. You may already know everything in this book, or you may consciously know very little about it. But something within you has been impressed by the crucial need to move in a more sacred and positive direction, and it is my hope that this book will go a long way towards making that happen. Once people are inspired, they'll move on their own and make the necessary changes, include the larger thoughts that would help them to change.

—Rebecca Field

Los Gatos, California

INTRODUCTION

THE COSMOS IS BOTH INSIDE AND OUTSIDE

Many people look into the starry heavens at night and wonder, "What is the purpose of it all?" Is it just meaningless lights in the sky, some arbitrary mixture of elements a great distance away? Or is it an expression of something so sacred that we cannot put words to it? To my mind and imagination, the night sky is evidence of the presence of the holy. It is everywhere, and is laden with meaning in every dimension of our lives.

Only as the years passed did I realize that the cosmos is both inside and outside, that it is the presence of order and beauty. It is as much in your heart and my heart as it is in the vastness of space dotted at night with stars and planets. The *outside* is the easy part. It is the sheer magnificence of a starry night. It leads us to relate things we know and are familiar with in our everyday environment. It can be measured, its chemistry analyzed, its density considered. It can be navigated. Meaning can be gleaned from it. It is the celestial stuff that the starship YOU accelerated through.

After many years I came to understand—to know—that the Truth, Beauty, and Goodness that humankind seems always to pursue is really within. The *insideness* is what the human heart is made of and created for, and the mind easily navigates in all directions.

While all living things are connected in some wonderfully mysterious way, clearly the all-embracing *outer space*, with its galaxies and multiple universes, is no different from our *inner space*, where there is justice, proportion, and harmony. In fact, the outer space can serve as a guide to self-understanding. For instance, if life—with all its preciousness and all its myriad forms—is to continue, then harmony must rule. And from harmony springs the elegant beauty of natural forms.

Marcus Aurelius (121-180 C.E.) taught that ethical action must arise from our understanding of the cosmos. And so ethics brings us into a cross-over area where both the inner and outer cosmos meet, greet, impregnate, and nurture each other, and create something new for the evolutionary flow.

Each of us has a great part to play in the evolution of humanity. To do so, we must know who we truly are—the divine wellspring from which we come, and the qualities of mind, heart, and soul that we can develop. The cross-fertilization of the *cosmos* (the outer universe that we see at night) with the *kosmos* (the human ability to be sensitive and create order and beauty; to know who we are and to co-create) involves risk. Yet when we are willing to face the important questions about each kind of grand identity possible for each of us, we have the potential of gaining dignity, authenticity, and freedom.

Antonio Machado puts poetic light on our identity:

> It doesn't matter now if the golden wine
> floats abundantly in your crystal cup,
> or if the bitter juice clouds the pure glass....
> You know the secret passageways
> of the soul, the roads that dreams take,
> and the calm evening
> where they go to die....
> There the good and silent spirits
> of life are waiting for you,
> and one day they will carry you
> to a garden of eternal spring.

from Times Alone, Passages in the House and Other Poems

by Antonio Machado

"Evolutionary cosmology" is an all-inclusive term that simultaneously encompasses a magnificent cosmos full of galaxies, other universes, and our solar system. The photographs taken through the Hubbell Telescope have made it possible for us to discover the unimaginable beauty and grandeur that surround us. The quantum world that we are entering suggests that everything in known creation is a unified whole, and is connected. More than anything, cosmology is about relationships—all kinds of connections—and includes the forces and energies within every human. And if it is about our kinship with everything, it is also about synthesis, about Oneness, about spirit, and about love that pervades all things.

In our near-catastrophic time, evolutionary cosmology has a lot to teach us. It reminds us that we have utterly forgotten the higher, natural order that wants to prevail on the Earth—a higher order that is seen in nature. It is humanity's task to remember the divine order and bring it into nature, or to co-create a higher third entity that includes both spirit and nature—and then to live by its higher rule. To pursue life without the awareness of the cosmic intelligence and love is to abandon our purpose on earth.

Our central calling is to take the most difficult risk imaginable for humans—to go beyond the ego and the haggard status quo that upholds economic, political, religious, and governmental edicts, which always dictate that we pay attention to their interests, and not to our own souls or to the music that wants to play in our hearts. It is so hard to do this because of the weight of the ego, which wants to be in control. It will not tolerate forays into the sacred, nor will it tolerate the awareness that we are part of a larger field of consciousness, created within the cosmos to manifest a higher Ground.

Thus *it is the human task to reignite the fire of the cosmos and choose to remember the spiritual, the good, the true, and the beautiful.* There is a terrible price to pay if we don't: the material order of the world will collapse. *Our great work as humans is to bring the sacred into balance with the material.*

After all—they are one!

THE PERENNIAL PHILOSOPHY

"If one is not oneself a sage or saint, the best thing one can do, in the field of metaphysics, is to study the works of those who were, and who, because they had modified their merely human mode of being, were capable of a more than merely human kind and amount of knowledge."

—From the Introduction to *The Perennial Philosophy*, by
Aldous Huxley

"*The Perennial Philosophy* is an attempt to present this Highest Common Factor of all theologies by assembling passages from the writings of those saints and prophets who have approached a direct spiritual knowledge of the Divine...."

—From the cover text, *The Perennial Philosophy*, 1946
British edition

For thousands of years, we have been heir to a tradition of the Ancient Wisdom. Expressed in legends, myths, mysteries, and archetypes with their captivating stories, puzzles, and labyrinths, this Ancient Wisdom has given rise to a philosophical system that turns out to be similar all over the world. Christianity has its roots in it, as do Islam and Judaism. Likewise, the Eastern religions can claim it as their foundation. Through it, all the great religious practices are linked.

One would think we would all be aware of it, even base how we live our lives on it as best we can. But the problem is that over time, this olden and *concealed* way of thinking has gone so far beneath the surface that relatively few people in the world are even aware that it exists.

What has come to be called the "Perennial Philosophy" was first written down about twenty-five centuries ago. But it is far older than that. For instance, the Buddha was alive and working in Asia at that time. It was the period of the Golden Age of Greece, when Plato, Socrates, and Pericles gave forth their wisdom.

This ancient philosophy has found many expressions, and has served as the underground river that has nourished all the great religious systems of today. It is to be found in the Vedanta, and in Hebrew prophecy. The Platonic dialogues are full of the wisdom of this way of thought. It is to be found in the Tao Te Ching. The Gospel of St. John contains it. The Mahayana Buddhist theology is an expression of it. Plotinus was an exponent of the ancient wisdom. Persian Sufis and Christian mystics were familiar with it.

Aldous Huxley—one of the modern philosophers to think about and elaborate upon it—wrote, in his book of the same name, that the Perennial Philosophy is imbedded in the traditions of all the "higher religions." The Perennial Philosophy is the highest and perhaps the best common factor linking the various belief systems on earth. All the great religions have tried over time to describe the same inchoate idea. Huxley, in his quest to articulate it for the modern era, discovered four fairly simple fundamental doctrines that quintessentially describe it:

1. The material world and individualized consciousness is the manifestation of the Absolute, within which all smaller realities are a part and without which they would not exist.

2. Human beings can know about the Absolute and have direct intuitive experience of it. The power of this kind of knowledge is so great that the one who experiences it *knows* he is one with the Absolute.

3. The experience is possible because humans are endowed with a dual nature: (a) an ego that is built to deal with and enjoy the phenomenal world, and (b) the Soul or the inner human being, so constructed to be at one with the Absolute. People have a choice which to identify with—the lower ego and the material world, or the Soul, which has the same nature as the Absolute or Spirit.

4. The purpose of human life is to identify with the Soul or the Higher Self and come to unified knowledge of the Absolute.

Looking a bit more deeply, here is what we find:

The *first principle of the Ancient Wisdom*—"*The material world and individualized consciousness is the manifestation of the Absolute, within which all smaller realities are a part and without which they would not exist*"—is that **there is One, and**

One is all there is. This is the underlying Reality for everything in the Cosmos. It is everywhere and in everything. Humankind, therefore, is left with a choice of living the life of the ego (the lower separated self—very much a part of the material world, with its glamours and desire nature always pulling and pushing for what it wants), or the life of the Soul. In choosing to identify with the Soul, we eventually align with, experience, and know God. Many fundamentalist versions of the great religions devote their efforts to persuading their followers to believe in the personal aspects of the One (such as God as a punitive Father). Yet while that has validity and meaning for many, in the Perennial Philosophy, the Absolute (or whatever one wants to call It) is the underlying Principle or Reality behind and beyond the personal aspects of God.

The *second principle of the Ancient Wisdom—"Human beings can know about the Absolute and have direct intuitive experience of it. The power of this kind of knowledge is so great that the one who experiences it knows he is one with the Absolute"*—advocates the realm of metaphysics and the knowledge of the heart. It suggests that we would do well to replace the ego-driven small mind with the wisdom that comes from the experiential knowledge of who we truly are. The primary quality of this experiential knowledge is based on the authenticity of love, where freedom and creativity reside. Once experienced it is plain to see that everything is connected and affects everything else.

The *third principle of the Ancient Wisdom—"The experience is possible because humans are endowed with a dual nature: (a) an ego that is built to deal with and enjoy the phenomenal world, and (b) the Soul or the inner human being, so constructed to be at one with the Absolute. People have a choice which to identify with:* *the lower ego and the material world, or the Soul, which has the* *same nature as the Absolute or Spirit"*—affirms **the dual nature of humanity**. To reach the Divine, we have to learn to live in constant self-sacrifice (not in a morbid or morose sense, but in the sense of using consciousness to make holy/make whole) and compassion for others. All religions teach that our personality—our identification with the ego and with materialism—is what prevents us from being aware of the higher part of our nature, the Soul. Once we have experienced Oneness, we go through the inner transformation and understand that we are part of, and have a certain responsibility for the unfurling of the cosmos.

And the *fourth principle of the Ancient* Wisdom—*"The purpose of human life is to identify with the Soul or the Higher Self and come to unified knowledge of the Absolute"*—addresses the purpose of human life. Humanity has come to think that external circumstances are more important than internal states of mind (especially with the advent and growth of industrialization). The purpose of life has come to mean activity: "What do you *do?*" Contemplation has fallen by the wayside, and the question of who we really are never comes up. Yet during the great Golden Ages of the past, in the glorious days of Greece, India, and China, for example, the quest for Truth—inner Truth—was all that mattered. After all, humans are cosmically 'engineered' to receive and apply the cosmos they experience in the world and in service to others.

In modern times, the Perennial Philosophy is expressed in all the great religions, though usually twisted and distorted by the mass mind that does not understand or wisely use the four main precepts. The ancient tradition is marked by an emphasis on inner truth, the language and music of the heart. The philosophy has birthed knowledge about all aspects of life which are within and behind outer appearances. The living wisdom gained from this perspective does not come through our egos and mastering facts, learning academically, or doing things in the outer world. Radical experientialism defines the philosophy of peak spiritual experience. It is not physical understanding but the knowledge of the heart, which we acquire as our consciousness touches, comes into contact with, and realizes the tremendous energy that comes from the highest sources.

If we are fortunate enough to have this experience, the world of meaning comes to life. We are not particularly occupied by the mechanical form. Instead, we become interested in the soul—spiritual—aspect of life. We are no longer trapped by the ego and its captivation with the material world and with money, possessions, power or fame.

Why the soul? It is the mediating principle between spirit and matter. It makes us who we are as individuals. The soul is behind the manifestation of the body, emotions, and mind. Because of its inclusive nature, the soul enables the personality to be creative, skillful, and more real as the central part of our being.

The Perennial Philosophy often mentions those who are *incarnations of the Absolute*—Masters of Humanity who have the capacity and grace to help us achieve our evolutionary goals. These very special people have shown up at various times and places, and know who they are. Because they possess such very significant inner knowledge, they can remind others of what has been forgotten when the small self's concerns win out over the Soul's. In our time, we may benefit by reminding ourselves that it is the practice of the Perennial Philosophy that makes us good Christians, good Buddhists, good Hindus, good Jews, good Taoists, good Muslims, and the like.

We all seek peace. We are all at different stages of spiritual development, and this is a good thing for the world. Because we each see things differently and uniquely, we can expose others to different viewpoints and be open to different viewpoints, ourselves. Peace will come when we are capable of accepting a more meaningful philosophy—a philosophy that includes the stirrings of the Cosmos, the breath of Life, and the brilliance of Love.

The length of time the Perennial Philosophy has been with us, its depth and breadth and global manifestation, has made it a practical way to live. With its guidance, we try to know and understand ourselves and our uniqueness. We try to listen to the small voice within. We examine our motives every day. In our effort to be in harmony with our inner reality, we learn to focus our mind rather than to be swayed and conditioned by our emotions. We meditate daily. We look for meaningful connections between events and the whole. We serve humanity and the planet in any and every way we can, whether it is a genuine smile to a stranger, working to feed the hungry or preventing the spread of AIDS. True religion depends on its practice.

"There is no religion higher than Truth."

—Soren Kirkegaard

PART I

THE PROMISE,
THE URGENCY OF THE TIME,
AND THE OPPORTUNITY

CHAPTER 1
COSMIC EVOLUTION

"The universe is a cosmos
containing within it the perfection of the order
of nature, beauty, and harmony."

—Pythagoras[1]

Whenever I go outside at night and see the stars, my mind gently takes me back to an experience I had long ago with a school chum in eighth grade. What she said has never left me.

My family had a cabin in the mountains of Colorado. One weekend, Frances came up to the cottage with me. After the sun went down, we walked until we found a favorite boulder of mine. Two natural seats in a weather-carved boulder beckoned us. Even in the starlight, we could see the snowy crests of Mount Evans, one of Colorado's towering mountain giants, looming to the west.

Knowing that Frances had taken on the starry skies as a hobby, I asked her to tell me about the stars. With all the usual layers of secrecy, falsehood, and arrogance from our life at school peeled off, she pointed out and named some of the constellations. She knew distances, too. This one was so many light years away. That one was a planet and was closer than the rest.

Then she said something that amazed me, something that I never would forget, something I have never heard since.

"I sometimes feel," she confided, "that the stars are my brothers and sisters, my parents, aunts, uncles and cousins. I love them as members of my family. It is almost as if they talk to me."

On that special evening, which, in a way, was not special at all, both my friend and I had an "Ah-ha!" experience—a sense of the spiritual, unlimited wholeness and its all-pervasiveness. What happened that night was not commonplace; and yet it could have happened anytime! (It still can.) Stars and cosmos became the source of a higher experience. That should be the goal of all of our human encounters.

Humans have a longing to reach out—even to the stars—and to embrace them, to listen to them, and to learn from them. Our experience of the cosmos transcends even our mental understanding. There is a feeling component that accompanies our awareness of the vastness of space, and the presence, perhaps, of other beings far out there with whom we can communicate. Surely, the lights that play against the black sky justify through us the reason for human existence. They come into being not so much through some thunderous "Big Bang" lost in the shrouds of time, but through their own desire to reveal themselves, to reach out, to co-create, and even to be one with us.

What happened in my consciousness, when I grasped—just a little bit—that I was connected in some way to these distant beings of light? I felt a sense of order, purpose, and perfection. Here, in the immense blackness lighted by the scattered stars, was the totality of the Good, the True, and the Beautiful.

Only many years later had life given me enough tests, sufficient allures, abundant failures, and many varied experiences that I can, in this book, attempt to flesh out my old awareness from that starry night in the Colorado mountains that the cosmos and everything in it was my brother. In that deep encounter with the roots of life itself, I now see that we all are part of an immense plan, infinite love, and a boundless creative process.

I am old now, and realize that I have always been in love with the cosmos.

I have been drawn to the subject of cosmic evolution throughout my adult life, and even earlier, because it represented totality—wholeness. It took in everything. It was big—really big—and constantly changing. Pictures of outer space from the Hubbell Telescope were beautiful: spiral galaxies, towering gasses, a panoply of light so beautiful that it took my breath away. Seeing a light-filled galaxy was like seeing everything all connected, proof that it all is one. Looking up at the visible cosmos also showed me presence of the macrocosm and the microcosm, each the reflection of the other.

Though I was not intimately familiar with the science behind the discoveries about the cosmos, the Perennial Wisdom had a strong inner meaning that intuitively illuminated things for me. It gradually dawned on me that I was an evolutionary cosmologist. This was the first time in my life that I felt such a strong identification. I felt a complete unity with all this grandeur contained within space. As my childhood friend said, "The stars are my brothers." There was a complete unity between the spiraling galaxies, the black holes and me. There was no separation, no difference; and the light in the cosmos, its movement and change, offered more than complete and joyous freedom. It also signaled the beginning of real responsibility. (Freedom and responsibility are one, like two sides of a coin. Both exist in consciousness. Both are to be carried out in everyday life.)

In its early stages, evolution proceeds very slowly. As time goes on, it gradually gets faster and faster. Once humankind came onto the scene, our initial development was very lengthy. But because of the potential inherent in our nature, our distant ancestors went through many subjective shifts. In time, humans were strongly affected by the cultures and civilizations that they built and lived in.

In the past several hundred years, the idea of evolution has been drastically misunderstood and argued about. Currently, evolution is understood as a discernible path at the physical level, with obvious stages and developments. Yet from the perspective of the Ancient Wisdom, evolution is a mental process of identifications with universal and inclusive ideas that enable humankind and life on the planet to move ahead so that identity with the Whole—the One—can be recognized. As the evolutionary process unfolds, people gradually come to recognize the presence of light in matter, in the etheric body—as shown through instinct, the intellect, the soul, and the intuition.

The path of human evolution goes from lower to higher—through the mineral, vegetal, and animal realms closer and closer to spirit. Evolution is a mental process, moving first from instinct, then through the intellectual phase, and then finally into the intuitive realm, where unity can more easily be perceived and experienced. It is the active intuition that enables us to sense the presence of the soul within the personality.

At first, when we are still in the instinctual realm, desire predominates, seeking all the allures of the material world. Then, as the soul becomes more aware, we often experience a conflict between spirit and matter. Eventually, we develop the conscious awareness of the unity and sacredness of all the parts. Finally, we find that we are not separate; and we know, without doubt, that our individual will is no longer a function of our separated ego, but an intrinsic, essential part of the divine Will. Then, in a very real sense, we move from light to light, from revelation to revelation, and from awareness to awareness—from lower nature to higher nature—until we arrive at the realm of life itself.

At each stage, something that was hidden is revealed, as if a powerful searchlight has been trained on these higher-level realms with which we now identify. And a succession of revelations occur and open humanity—first to the environment

23

and the material world, then to the world of ideals, then to the nature of the soul, of ideas—and finally, to the One.

At our current stage of evolution, most of humankind is engulfed and swamped by emotions. Eventually, we learn to use the light of the mind, rather than the emotions. The light of the mind flows from the soul into the personality. Once we learn to use the mind to dissolve negative emotions before they take deadly hold of us, we are on the way to better health, a happier life, freedom and the next-higher rung on the evolutionary ladder. From the vantage point of where most of us are now in an evolutionary sense, the task is immense—and there is no doubt that we shall ultimately be successful!

CHAPTER 2

THE COSMIC BREATH
THE NEW STORY OF THE
COSMOS THAT INCLUDES
YOU AND ME

Many people look into the starry heavens at night and wonder, "What is the purpose of it all?" Is it just meaningless lights in the sky, some arbitrary mixture of elements a great distance away? Or is it an expression of something so sacred that we cannot put words to it? To my mind and imagination, this is evidence of the presence of the holy. It is everywhere, and is laden with meaning in every dimension of our lives.

The purpose of the cosmos is about the breath—the in-breath and the out-breath—just as much as it is about human expansion of consciousness. In many ways, the unfolding of the cosmos parallels human evolution. Cosmos and human contain one another.

25

The Scientific View and the Spiritual View

Humanity is now between the two towers of the suspension bridge that will, if we choose, lead to a better and kinder life than we now know—or to devastation and unimaginable degradation everywhere—with one tower representing scientific materialism and the other standing for a more introspective and open approach to life. Somehow our task is to erect a third supporting structure in our bridge to the future and our salvation, a system that embodies the best parts of science and also includes the sacred dimension of life. It cannot be otherwise. The materialistic bent of civilization, while it has brought many gifts, has fallen short of what we seek.

When we contemplate the cosmos, we tend to think in terms of a "Big Bang." *Was* there a big bang? Who knows? Humans seem to need to believe there was a beginning point to all of life. Science teaches us that the cosmos had a moment of beginning and likewise will have an instant of ending. Believing that gives us some comfort, some assurance that there is an order in things (in spite of science's denial that there is a cosmic purpose). But suppose that what we call the Big Bang is just one in a series of cosmic breaths? What if our universe—and we, ourselves—are *always* being created or we constantly co-create ourselves?

Astronomer Fred Hoyle spoke of "continuous creation," constant cosmic creation, without beginning or end. Even though his ideas run counter to those of the scientific establishment, his concept better fits a spiritual viewpoint. Science does not generally include a spiritual perspective, being about the material world. Strict, accepted scientific method bases itself on a series of largely undisputed theories. Scientists accept the Big Bang theory as the foundation of the cosmos. They postulate that the universe began as an infinitely hot initial singularity, expanding and cooling according to Einstein's theories of gravitation and relativity.

We all derive huge benefits from scientific achievement, and need to be aware of its blessings as well as limitations. One significant limitation is the scientific assumption, or credo, that only the material world exists, thus making the spiritual dimension non-existent. What scientists don't realize is that *behind the phenomenal world is a subtle world, where all the energy is.*

Creativity Is a Constant

The theory of continuous creation rests on the basic cosmological assumption that the universe did not evolve over time; rather, it always *has* existed and always *will* exist in the future. This is the *perfect cosmological principle.* One might think that leads to the conclusion that the cosmos is static, and that nothing much goes on. But this is hardly the case!

The whole-systems viewpoint teaches us that that life in the material world is connected with all phases of evolution. What about the evolution of the *non-*material, *subtle,* and *spiritual* world? Physicist Erich Jantsch, who believes in the immediacy of existence, says that evolution requires us to take into account the presence of *re-ligio* (the root-meaning of *religion,* to re-connect),

27

linking backward to the origin. He also says, "letting that be the main spiritual concern, it is also becoming the core of creative action."[1]

The radiation of energies beyond our understanding is the starting point for *the harnessing of cosmic energies.* Energies constantly pour into the individual from a myriad of sources. Whether they are internal, external, or a combination of both, we are constantly bombarded by all kinds of forces. Many are so subtle that they are far beyond our recognition. They tend to be positive in nature and to support life and the expansion of consciousness on many levels. By means of these energies, discoveries are made (such as the means of using electricity, and a thousand other discoveries) when pressures build from the heart of the cosmos and impact human minds. There, we receive impressions. The impressions keep coming until we have to do something about them and bring them to life in some way.

And so we see that humanity's purpose is two-fold:

1. To know God (aka, the Divine, Wholeness, Allah, Oneness, the Great Whizzbang, Source, Jahweh, Ram, the One), or whatever you want to call It);

2. To realize that humans have the unique ability to be creative.

Human creativity is love in action, and springs from the heart. It also equates with freedom, according to Russian philosopher Nicolas Berdyaev. Thus:

love = creativity = freedom

or

creativity = love = freedom

or

freedom = creativity = love.

Our endless inspiration and need to be inventive is the impetus behind evolution, culture, and our responsibility for designing and implementing our own transformation.

Of the three attributes, "freedom" may be the most difficult to understand. Freedom is a synonym for *responsibility*—that is, the ability to be responsive; and until we really take that in, we are lost. When we cannot be responsive to what calls to us from within our heart, we cannot be responsible to it, and so we cannot truly be free. We search for joy and happiness everywhere imaginable, except in the place where it is to be found—within our heart, and through a life of service to others.

And yet, vast numbers of people all over the world are finding this freedom, as they discover causes to serve that match their inner calling.

The Awakening Collective Soul

In Paul Hawken's book *Blessed Unrest*, he presents a vision of a global movement that has erupted spontaneously all over the world in the last few years. It has no center, no originator; no one is in charge. Rather, these are grass-roots interest groups that burst forth—often as a nonprofit organization, or through a kind

29

act by someone who cares and does something that makes a difference in another's life. It is not about serving the ego. It is about kinship and the recognition that we are all family. The actual numbers of organizations and people involved are beyond counting, so nobody knows how big the group is. It is happening everywhere, and could almost be compared to a "Big Bang," itself.

Hawken believes it is indicative of the coming world—part of the new story of the cosmos that includes you and me. If there is a center at all, it is the human heart, wherever in the world it is in touch with need and taking responsibility for it. This growing tendency is an early indication of the presence of the awakening collective Soul, or the principle of love in action within humanity.

People are now catching a glimpse of the fact that *humanity is the hope, the promise, and the keeper of all evolutionary processes.* In fact, the human race is the key to the stage-by- stage unfolding of evolution. The greater collective of humankind— people like you and me—can function as "creative seeds" on various planes of cosmic existence and contain and express some aspect of evolving divine consciousness.

We live in a time when free will and goodwill must prevail, if we are to survive. Goodwill involves human's responsibility to human. It also requires that we freely choose a positive relationship to divine purpose, and understand the divine intention of love as the central purpose of creation at this time. This means that we must participate in every phase of life, and be consciously involved in every moment possible.

Each of Us Has a Special Place in the Evolution of Humanity and Humanity Has a Special Place in Creation

As consciousness is related to some kind of sensitivity, the particular nature of an individual's consciousness will suggest in what way he or she can serve this evolution. For instance, some who are particularly tuned into beauty may be artists, while others who think more abstractly may be mathematicians. Those who are able to sense beings, structures, and ideas in the subtle world carry within them the vessel of the potentiality for greater consciousness on some particular level of divine activity and the great divine plan, which expresses the one purpose through time and space.

Astronomers tell us that each one of us has stardust in our bodies—that particles from the "Big Bang" (if that theory is to be believed) are actually part of our physical bodies. Assuming that much of the cosmos is filled with life in one form or another, then over time many of these particles, atoms, and molecules have been—are now—or will be human beings. Humanity thus has a special place in creation, and a definite, clear responsibility to carry out certain tasks to further the higher plan.

Opening the Gate to Spiritual Energy

If humanity holds the key to the fulfillment of the divine Plan, then it is we—all of us—who must initiate what needs to happen. And the gate we are destined to open is to *spiritual* energy. (This seems obvious, in light of the rampant materialism currently abounding all over the earth.) People all over the world are

31

responding to sacred energy. This response comes from every diverse culture and racial mixture. It arises from people who belong to every religion and political ideology. It issues forth from the educated and uneducated, alike.

The gate to spiritual energy is not light-years away. It is close. It is always there, just waiting to be unlocked. It is humanity's prerogative to open the gate—or to leave it closed, as we have done for roughly the past 500 years, in our hypnotic infatuation with materialism. Materialism became prevalent in human life with the adoption of science as our all-defining god. Materialism took over our monolithic systems—government, education, social management, and the like—and corrupted them with greed, sense-indulgences, and a "me-first" attitude. Humankind has put a huge amount of energy into improving material life over the last half-millenium of human history. This has been a necessary step in our growth of consciousness; there is nothing wrong with it. The problem is that we have allowed the forces of materialism to atrophy and stiffen to the point that, at present, people have no values by which to help them find their way *except* materialistic values. We have lost our sense of balance. We have forgotten that both spiritual and material values can and must exist side by side.

Humankind's purpose now is to shift this reductive, terribly confining focus; to unlock, release, and express the spiritual energies of Light, Love, and Will. We are called to shift our consciousness in a new direction—towards an unstoppable spiritual impetus that *includes* the material aspects of life but without glorifying them above all else.

It is the challenge of the generations now living to include and live these two values—the material and the spiritual—simultaneously and in balance, joyously. Doing so might well bring the greatest efflorescence of the arts the world has ever known. Every department of human life would be positively affected. Women and men would experience justice, and human rights would be respected, perhaps even increased.

As humanity turns toward spiritual values, holistic ideals like the quest and movement toward unity, integrated and joyful group work and the understanding of inner essence will be primary. We will recognize the presence of something higher in us all—the Soul, qualities indicating the presence of God within each one of us; the shining Light within whose guidance, when followed, offers the realized human hope of promise and glory.

The Key Lies Within

If humanity is to carry out its destiny, we will have to center our attention within. Only then will we be able to unbolt the lock on the gate that leads to higher kingdoms, and release the powers and beauties of the Soul so they can be expressed in everyday life. *It is in our hands to use our Soul qualities to build a better world.* We can use materialism—not in the separating way that it is being used now, but in a way that allows the energies of light and love to express freely in the world.

Eleanor Roosevelt exemplifies the constructive use of both material and spiritual energies. She raised a large family, and had to deal with the deaths of most of her kin: her mother; her father; her uncle, President Theodore Roosevelt; her son; and eventually, her husband, Franklin Delano Roosevelt. Despite being surrounded by tragedy, her desire to serve humanity was so great that she became a part of the United Nations in its infancy, and helped write the Universal Declaration of Human Rights. She became the chairwoman of the Human Rights Commission, worked hard to eradicate racial prejudice and discrimination, and spent much time helping the poor and downtrodden. By serving humanity, she had one foot in the material world and the other in the spiritual world.

People everywhere sense the need for change. All kinds of actions are taking place on all sorts of levels. Each of us is uniquely qualified to do *something*. Nothing short of a planetary revolution is needed—a total *socio-geo-transformation*—in order to positively address the state of the world and its inhabitants, which currently is so serious that life itself is threatened. When we can let go of "me"-driven interests, and instead accept that each one of us is both the center and the ground of necessary change, this all encompassing transformation will happen. The Source—the One—is at the center; and material living (necessary as it is) revolves around God and cannot ever take God's place.

To find the key to the essential and transformative gate, we need to focus our awareness on the *inner* dimensions of life—on the Soul, the Buddha or Christ consciousness—and use the material world as the playground of our redemptive activity.

CHAPTER 3

THE IMPENDING WORLD CATASTROPHE (A WARNING WE CAN HEED— AND TRANSFORM)

TRANSFORMING THE PLANETARY CRISIS

I attended a conference where former astronaut Edgar Mitchell was a speaker. It was electrifying. He's in his 70s, now, or maybe more. He's become very humble.

As he spoke, he put his clenched fist in front of his face, no more than 6–8 inches from his eyes. Then he said that after all the work following the moon landing was done, he finally had time to look out at the earth—and it was no bigger than his fist. This whole earth! This blue jewel, just hanging there in the blackness of space!

I think that's very touching. Because, as another astronaut said, "Everything that means anything to us happens down on that tiny blue ball. This earth is so incredibly beautiful. And we are just making havoc with it."

We face a unique challenge on our planet, today—probably the most difficult and serious one in human history. Nothing of such stupendous magnitude has happened to humanity in its roughly 250,000 years of existence. The crisis is on every front and in every area of our lives. The time when we can ignore it is past. It is so vast that it affects everyone alive today, in one way or another.

It is time to wake up!

Most people already are aware that humankind faces a crisis of unprecedented proportions. In all our known history, never before has there been a crisis that has affected the entire earth and all life on it. It involves every dimension of human life—from the political, educational, economic, and religious arenas, to healthcare and wellness—even the food we eat—as well as all other domains of life. For example:

- Forms of energy that we have relied upon are called into question, as we hear the dire prediction of the death of the Gulf of Mexico due to an offshore drilling mistake.

- The planet is covered with polluted air, causing serious illness.

- Poverty is strident and is beginning to affect wealthier, first-world countries. There are huge differences between the lives of the rich and the poor, and the deprivation explodes other problems. Millions do not have adequate shelter or even any housing at all. They lack available clean drinking water, and live in poverty so enveloping that many never have enough to eat.

- In some of the wealthy countries, obesity is a serious health problem.

- Mental illness is a galloping and uncontrolled social problem.

- Prisons are filled to overflowing. The crime rate in some cities is so high that the police turn their backs on it.

- Sadly, we have allowed Western society to honor the profane in everything, to the point where the sacred is not recognized, or for all intents and purposes no longer exists. Religious fundamentalism, whether Christian, Islamic Jewish, Hindu, Buddhist, or some other sect, is rampant, intolerant, and separatist by nature.

- Genocide continues in Tibet and Darfur, as well as other countries.

- The profit motive and a consumer-driven culture leave us unsatisfied and yearning for something else, though we don't know what that might be.

- The world is so filled with noise that people seek quiet and silence in retreat centers, far away from commercial bustle.

- We face institutional corruption, and find that leaders have betrayed the people they have sworn to protect.

- Pharmaceutical companies dominate the health industry and can be as destructive as they are helpful; people have come to depend on test-tube fixes that make a few rich, instead of using natural remedies that are not very expensive (or profitable for the pharmaceutical companies).

The list goes on. We could add to it for weeks.

The overall problem is a crisis in values. The unexamined prevailing philosophy of our time is the societal belief in materialism, mechanistic thinking, logical positivism, and a pessimistic existentialism. We have lost sight of older ways of valuing the world, such as the integral, mystical, and neo-Vedantist approaches. Over the last 150 years or more, we have witnessed the progressive decay of society.

The Transformative Tide

We must realize that there are reasons why we face so many varied problems simultaneously. The causes lie in humankind's remote past. They go so far back in time that there are no written records. To many, the causes have no meaning because we have little understanding of the nature of very early humanity. Yet at the same time that decadence, with its lack of values, is out of control, the opposite is beginning to emerge. To understand the future, we must have a feeling for what has gone before— because something wonderful is unfolding in humanity.

First, we must understand that our next evolutionary steps require huge changes in attitude about everything conceivable. Many people are now taking the initiative and developing new and creative methods for us to live together in harmony and finding new ways we can care deeply about our planet and take care of it. Amidst the waves of moral irresponsibility, young people in particular are doing something to turn the tide. They volunteer to help people in a variety of ways, from providing transportation, to helping senior citizens, to building housing for the financially strapped, and much more.

The evolutionary unfolding of humanity is a major cause for our current predicament. The intelligence within humans is so strongly awakened and vital that nothing can stop our forward movement. The things we know and are on the verge of knowing can be applied for selfish ends with resultant great pain; or they can be applied for benevolent ends, that serve us all. Our challenge is to develop a spiritual value system. Among the most needed qualities humankind must develop are purpose, dedication and that faithfulness to a group's cause that integrates the members. Steadfastness to high and enduring principles is a living testament in healing disagreements with co-workers. One of the most needed qualities humankind must develop is group loyalty to a long-term purpose.

Many people are starting to operate as a unified whole within themselves. The personality—with its soul, and its mind, emotions, and brain—works in unison in an integrated person. The higher octave of these forces—wisdom, love, and direction—are yet to be developed. When we look around, we see women and men who are intelligent and well-trained, and who embody their realized integration. They are capable of acting as intelligent and idealistic people, capable of varying degrees of leadership. These people work in every field of human endeavor and contribute much in their area. They have an effect on civilization and, equally, imprint their culture. Many have sound motives, yet are not experienced in the ways of the soul and make many errors. Still, their long-term effect is to stimulate public awareness, and that has many benefits for all of us.

While it is true that we have experienced terrorism, brutality, rising crime, and the demoralization of people brought on by war and genocide, inspiring altruism exists at the same time. The Occupy Movement, for example, is significant because it has spread like a wildfire all over the world. People in 2,600 cities around the world "Occupy" in their locations for justice and fair treatment of the 99% who do not have the wealth, power, and privileges of the 1% who do. Other organizations have been instituted to abolish war; aid the poor and get them into a position of self-sufficiency; end hunger; build needed housing; supply clean, safe drinking water; and end sex slavery, to name a few. The very long list of altruistic activities that groups are involved in is a stunning example of the human intention to live within the context of the will-to-good, to demonstrate practical concern for others, and to live with compassion and treat others as they would want to be treated.

THE MASTERS AND THE PLAN

The other side to all the negativity comes from thoughtful and sensitive people who have the good of humanity in mind, and who are guided by the Plan which embodies that aspect of divine Purpose which is able to be manifested in the world at a particular time. This is possible because it is infused with higher Will.

The Plan, contained in the Mind of the One, has the dynamic energy of consecutive ideas—whether physical, psychological, individual, planetary, spiritual, or cosmic—that manifest in evolution.

Over the last 500 years, spiritually aligned beings have come closer to the Earth to influence and advance human consciousness. These august personages, also known as the Masters,[4] operating from a perspective that reflects the Perennial Philosophy, have brought the seeds of world rescue and the hope of recovery to the world.

What has changed in the last 500 years, however, is that the "critical mass" of candidates for higher spiritual knowledge and responsibility has dramatically increased. The result is the increasing speed of life and the evolution of the Earth itself, as well as the increase in human awareness. The result is that humanity is ready to make an evolutionary leap! A group conversation that I was privileged to be part of arrived at a conference-born definition of "critical mass":

> A critical mass in human social terms is that group of people within a total population for whom a seed idea gains a certain amount of momentum. They are

prepared, responsible members of the community and are willing to create, empower, and sustain a new and needed paradigm. If critical mass is between 1 to 2 percent of the total population of seven billion now alive, then the critical mass in the world equals approximately 70,000,000.

A Magic Leap in Consciousness

What humanity needs now is a magic leap in consciousness—a very special moment when humanity has a widespread experience of, and acceptance of, the sacred. When that moment comes, a new world can be born. We will seek actual spiritual contact through the guidance of the Masters and the light of our own souls. When that awareness reaches a flash point—a moment of cosmic consciousness, *satori*, Japanese for enlightenment—then the Masters will no longer have to remain in the background.

But I am ahead of myself! Let me back up a step.

When a world-shaking event of towering spiritual dimension occurs, a new world can be born.

The idea of a leap in consciousness comes out of quantum mechanics. Physicist Eric Jantsch wrote in his book, *The Self-Organizing Universe:*

" ...the genealogical process of history may to some extent be overcome, ...implying that... whole structural platforms, whole civilizations, societal systems, art and life styles...must jump to a new structure. A pluralism emerges [in evolution] in

42

which many dynamic structures penetrate each other at the same level. In such a pluralism, there is no longer the familiar evolution in big step functions. Change, increasing in absolute measure, occurs not only vertically, in historical time, but also horizontally, in a multitude of simultaneous, processes, none of which necessarily has to assume destructive dimensions."[1]

This suggests that from the perspective of physics, evolution *usually* follows a self-reinforcing process. However, in *our* time, everything in planetary life is askew, off-kilter, and chaotic. Therefore, in order for humanity to continue to evolve, a critical mass of people must make a "quantum leap." Once this happens, the leap will create a fairly rapid shift in consciousness of enough people (who were not necessarily consciously working to make this shift) that whole systems will change into something quite different from what we have now. Some of the "leap" may be spontaneous (or appear to be). In the moment of the leap, some will not even question it, because it will be something that is called for from the heart of life itself in order for life to continue itself. If enough people take this leap, they will make a dramatic mental and heart-felt leap both to change themselves and to shift many of the systems or societal structures now in place all over the world. This change will be consistent with wise planetary living. These changes will include the following:

- We will treat our home planet with love and respect.

- We will address whole societies as if they mattered.

43

- We will create institutions that can nourish small groups and individuals at all levels of their being.

- At the same time, political systems will weaken and some will even disappear. Conceivably, the United States will no longer feel the need to be the monolithic guiding image for the world; and yet since some people in the U.S. will have made the leap, they will be open to new realities, which in turn will open the eyes of many others to the importance of true justice and respect for all.

- It will be increasingly evident that we are not isolated beings, but that we interpenetrate each other beyond theories and belief systems, so that our world views penetrate each other's.

- If values shift sufficiently in the direction of openness to the sacred, we will likely see an efflorescence of life and human culture—the arts, law, and so on—even more brilliant than that of ancient Greece or the Renaissance.

The Great Opportunity Facing Us

What do we—especially the spiritually inclined—have a responsibility to do? What can we take on that will encourage, precipitate, and enable such a stupendous change?

"Many are called, but few are chosen." In this case, this saying is true only because *we* choose *ourselves* to do the necessary work. No one chooses us. Endowed with free will, we can willingly and lovingly choose to give what light we can generate to the cosmos, for the love of humanity and the planet.

There is an opportunity now—an open door leading to a glorious future—that calls for our cooperation. The question is, are we ready to do the necessary work to make it happen? It is in our hands. The main work to be done at this time is to educate public opinion, and that takes work and sacrifice. If we are willing to cooperate with the Plan, then we each must answer the following questions as authentically as possible.

- Do I want to help establish a useful and meaningful interface between the spiritual and material worlds? If so, what can I do to make the connection a greater reality in the world and for others?

- How can I contribute to the linkage of the spiritual and material dimensions? What are my special experiences, talents, skills, interests? What more do I have in my life and circumstances to help in the way of meditation, understanding the Plan, and helping others?

Meditation, understanding, and love are what will turn the present rampant chaos and raging materialism around to a more positive direction for all of us. *Meditation* opens the mind to the next steps to take. *Understanding* is the basis for wisdom and helps us adapt to change, especially in the environment, and to other people as well as to new ideas and ways of living. Understanding arises from intuitive insights from within, which heed those special moments garnered from the spiritual dimension of life. It is this spiritual understanding that brings us to the level of desire. And

45

love releases the energy necessary to manifest the Plan in the world.

Seed Ideas

This is a time when humanity is beginning to receive seed designs for the future. These seeds are distinctive ideas, different in quality from ideas of the past. Their distinguishing characteristics express the energy traits of the Aquarian era into which humanity, our planet, and our solar system move.

Almost all the great ideas of the past that have succeeded in influencing and motivating people were gifts of intuitive men and women. This is how evolution on Earth occurs: inspired people grasp an idea that they intuit from a higher realm; change it into something that others can understand, mentally; and make it sufficiently desirable to capture people's attention. Then some creative person causes it to manifest, through the ability to coordinate the spiritual with the material. Such a person sees that the idea is part of the greater whole, so potentially alive within a society that it is the kernel of a major expansion of consciousness. Leonardo de Vinci and Michelangelo are examples of people who brought great ideas in this way. The rise of the computer is another example. Whole civilizations are affected by the revelation of ideas.

Groups as Seedbeds for Evolutionary Ideas

However, as humanity moves closer to the energetic expression of the Aquarian Age, evolutionary ideas will increasingly flow through *groups* rather than only through individuals. As we look around today, we find many who see the dream for the future. These people work together, form groups, and recognize each other, knowing themselves as souls because of their united understanding and because the light of knowledge, intellect, and intuition is clear to them. Sharing the same interests, they organize group activities; and so a bond unites them. The Internet, for example, reveals many groups like this. Occupy Wall Street is one example, and it has become global.

Evolution is evident as a culture and its resulting civilization becomes definable through art, literature, laws, government, and scientific achievements. The cultural developments of humanity increasingly reflect the presence of the mind and heart and their combined sensitivity to a higher Order. At the coming stage of humanity's evolution, spiritually inclined people all over the world readily respond to the mental stimulation of the unmistakable inspiration of intelligent love, especially in terms of developing intuitive abilities, an awareness of universality and inclusiveness, and the ability to understand and express spiritual ideas in the world and for humanity.

World-Servers Who Want to Contribute

The Masters realized that a bridging group was needed to bring about a change in human and planetary life—one that was not completely positive or negative, that would reflect its society of origin, and whose members would constitute a spectrum of humankind and be willing to play a more neutral role in the progress of human life. When world-servers transcend the usual polarities, a higher dimension of human life will burst forth into the cultures of the world.

A *culture* is different from a *civilization*. A *civilization* is a mass expression of consciousness as people live it out in their daily lives. The general attitude is negative. People don't like this or that. In contrast, a *culture* is expressed to a large extent by those who are mentally active, whose hearts are open and responsive; they are creative, positive, and respond to ideas that make sense in the everyday world. This group understands the link between the inner world of the soul and the outer, everyday life. Artistic creations are noteworthy expressions of a culture. In some cases, religious and political developments move many people to a higher grasp of inner Truth. Spiritually inclined people all over the world readily respond to mental stimulation, the inspiration of intelligent love. *Evolution* is evident in a culture, and its resulting civilization becomes definable through its art, laws, literature, and scientific achievements. Those who participate in a civilization gradually move on and take a more mentally active part in their culture.

And so a higher dimension came forth as the New Group of World Servers (NGWS), a name given them by the Master Djwal Khul and written about by his amanuensis, Alice Bailey. This group belongs to neither civilization nor to culture, but is better suited to play a more neutral role in the progress of human life. This group is a kind of grassroots global humanitarian movement taking on the eradication of injustice, inequality, and corruption. Organizations are springing up all over the world to turn things around. They are organic and rooted in life itself.

What does this tell us? That people want to contribute. They want to participate. They want something good for others to come from their efforts. This phenomenon is global and goes far beyond national, political, religious, sectarian, or sexual boundaries.

The groups of people who have a strong orientation to service nourish the starting point of a new world behind the scenes, and so are doing various things to pull societies in a more positive direction. Trained and experienced in various aspects of the work of the world, such as education and politics, they create a link between groups that are already active and the Masters. For example, one group may work futuristically to heal nations. Others may work to mend the environment or restore justice. Indeed, much of the "machinery" for healing on the planet is already in place. For example, the United Nations is actively present and works in almost all of the monolithic areas of human life. People gather together, work cooperatively, and share their ideas about every facet of human and planetary life imaginable. Some groups scan the political and military horizon looking for infringements and enlisting thousands of people to sign petitions to end, change, or start policies, laws, and ways of going about life that have served their purpose and must be dismantled and rebuilt again. This means creating laws to prevent the use of methyl iodide, a poisonous substance to put on strawberries; making regulations to monitor nuclear fallout; developing a strong and effective legal system to mandate that corporations pay for defiling the environment, and then cleaning it up. It means putting certain animal and plant species on the endangered list. It means that we have to start thinking and caring for all of it—people, the environment, animals, and plants. We are one, and we need each other.

Leaders emerge amidst the confusion of the tumultuous and threatening chaos in which much of humanity is now involved. Strong, insightful people such as the Dalai Lama and Wangari Maathai compel our attention. Able to make themselves heard, they speak in a new and needed voice, and command respect (though in some cases they are viewed with hatred and mistrust). The Dalai Lama speaks of the unity of all religions: "All major religious traditions carry basically the same message—that is, love, compassion, and forgiveness. The important thing is they should be part of our daily lives." Wangari Maathai, understood the importance of people and declared, "It is the people who must save the environment. It is the people who must make their leaders change. And we cannot be intimidated. So we must stand up for what we believe."

The *avant garde* lead with their thinking and actions, and masses of people carry out their ideas. Both these planetary leaders have influenced millions. The Dalai Lama has *lived* the unity of all religious traditions, and he is respected and honored throughout the world. As a result of his travels and public and private presentations, he has helped people face their problems and led the way to a much greater understanding of Tibetan Buddhism and the universal viewpoint it offers the world.

Similarly, Wangari Maathai founded the Green Belt movement in Africa, and planted lot of trees there, with the help of other women. She also concentrated on drawing attention to women's rights. She helped to raise the consciousness of people in Africa about the needs and rights of women.

World Servers are our great hope. This is not a named, formal group—indeed, many are in this group and don't realize it. Others, however, are aware, and they do what they can to promote solutions. These women and men (and *you* may be one!) are the midwives of a new and better future. Their vision enables the rest of us to be inspired, make our unique contribution, and give birth to a new civilization. These bright-eyed children of a new dawn will gradually bring about a new culture; and, importantly, a new viewpoint, inclined to universality and inclusiveness, as well as justice and life rights for those in all kingdoms (human, animal, vegetable, and mineral) inhabiting our planet. Many people are now taking the initiative and developing new and creative methods for us to live together in harmony, finding new ways that we can care deeply about and take care of our planet.

These groups of World Servers do not interfere with the peoples' beliefs or loyalties. They try to practice brotherhood and overlook racial differences, political antipathies, economic disparities, and religious ideologies. People in this group teach others to share voluntarily. They work with good-hearted people—those of goodwill who work with the principle of co-operation. As women and men realize the depth and breadth of our blood- and soul-relationship to one another, hatred and the feeling of being separate will disappear. People will take on a new sense of responsibility.

A Legacy of Building and Rebuilding Nations. Those who labor to rebuild nations labor conscientiously so that the Masters' ideas can be expressed in different countries. One stirring example of this in America's history took place at the time of the signing of the Declaration of Independence in Philadelphia on July 4, 1776. Every man present was emboldened because the Americans had won the Revolutionary War. (They all knew that they would have been subject to death for high treason, had the war been lost.) A new nation was being formed, and the men present did not all agree about what the modern country's policies should be.

On that memorable day, men like John Adams and Dr. Benjamin Franklin gave speeches. The afternoon was hot and muggy, and those who were to sign the document before them argued about the death penalty for traitors. They talked about scaffolds, axes and "the gibbet"—when an unknown man in the balcony stood up and cried out:

> "Gibbet! They may stretch our necks on all the gibbets in the land; they may turn every rock into a scaffold; every tree into a gallows; every home into a grave and yet the words of that parchment can never die! They may pour our blood on a thousand scaffolds, and yet from every drop that dyes the axe, a new champion of freedom will spring into birth! The British King may blot out the stars of God from the sky, but he cannot blot out His words written on

that parchment there. The works of God may perish: His words never!

"The words of the declaration will live in the world long after our bones are dust. To the mechanic in his workshop they will speak hope; to the slave in the mines freedom: but to the coward kings, these words will speak in tones of warning they cannot choose but hear...Sign that parchment. Sign....I would beg you to sign the parchment for the sake of those millions whose very breath is now hushed in intense expectation as they look at you for the ....words: God has given America to be free."

No one knew who the speaker was and he was never seen again. John Hancock rushed forward to take the pen and sign his name. The other signers quickly took the quill and signed their names.[2]

CHAPTER 4

A SPIRITUAL REASON FOR WORLD PROBLEMS

After approximately 250,000 years of human evolution, humanity is still a work in process. Our main personality attributes are still askew.

This is because the fundamental problem of humankind is *psychological.* The human race still finds itself befuddled and confused.

The problem is *internal* and manifests as:

- untamed brain responses;

- the spectrum of emotional responses (frequently unconscious and undirected); and

- mental events that may or may not actually have meaning.

Although our capacity to discern and differentiate is improving, it is still slow in developing. We require a better ability to discriminate correctly: to know the difference between what is more directly of God and what is simply materialistic; to understand the unfortunate cleavage between the sacred and the profane, especially in our extremely materialistic period. We have, in other words, a psychological split that needs to be made whole.

The psychological split that humans endure occurs in three areas:

1. within the individual;

2. between the mind and the lower nature, consisting of the physical body and the emotional field; and

3. between the emotions and the analytical mind.

The Split within the Individual

There is a gap between the lower emotional levels; i.e., negative, destructive emotions and the higher levels of the mind where we can think in universal and inclusive terms. When this split exists, the individual often has an inability to correctly discriminate between the sacred and the profane. The problem is that the mind is far greater than we tend to acknowledge. Until we recognize and use the universal mind within which gives direction, meaning and light, there will be a lack of clarity, confusion and the tendency to be separative.

The Split between Mind and Lower Nature: The Physical and Etheric Bodies

Some people are awake to the fact of the etheric body. The etheric is the subtle-yet-physical dimension of all physical objects. In humans, for instance, the etheric body is the subtle body that underlies the dense physical body that we are familiar with. We can see, touch, and measure the physical body, but most people cannot see the etheric body even though it is present with us all the time. In The Perennial Philosophy considers the etheric body to be our *true* form, since it is the framework to which the dense physical body conforms. It is through the etheric body that people are able to receive and integrate information about spiritual unity. The etheric body has tremendous power, if we can only recognize it. Then, we can consciously direct energy to and through it for healing, and use it to work with higher aspects of our being.

How Separativeness Touches Our Relation to the Larger World

Because of these internal psychological splits, there are deep cracks in *all* phases of our lives. For example, *the separation between humankind and the environment* is increasingly evident, Corporations ransack the planet and destroy lives for their own gain. Our current approach to the planet and its needs is blind, self-centered, and selfish. Most of us are not yet as kind and thoughtful to Mother Earth as we would be if we truly understood our connection to our planet, and what's at stake. Our sense of responsibility has yet to truly develop. Finally, *the divide we*

57

experience between the soul and the personality produces behavior that tends to be selfish and self-centered—which would not be true if we truly recognized our oneness, natural connectedness and interdependence.

The problems we have and the ramifications they have for humanity are staggering. However, there is no need for despair! I believe that humanity will solve the crisis—but not until we understand the causes from an energetic perspective. We must not forget that we are evolutionary beings and have experienced many crises in our long history as the human race—the only race that matters! Personal and societal challenges face everyone alive. Given our propensity for ego aggrandizement, lust for power, and conniving greed as some of our more serious flaws, we must not forget that the Hierarchy of Love acts on our behalf, leaving us with the hope and promise of a brighter future—as long as we learn the very difficult lessons that currently plague us. After all, we are all a contributing part of the present tribulations as well as being the source of bright expectations for the future (being ruled by divine thought through our energy bodies). The energy configuration within each of us bonds us to one another, and to all life and all life forms. We find we are all an integral part of the whole of creation. As we become increasingly aware of the mind of intelligent love and its importance, in time we will learn to bring our own minds into the sphere of the mind of the Divine, as it works and expresses through the Hierarchy of Love.

Awakening the Will

As long as we—humanity at large—become determined to take right action in the best way we know how, true positive evolution can and will take place. However, we will require the power of our awakened will in order to overcome the problem. We must all prepare to engage in the mission to rescue and liberate humanity. We are one, in spirit and in Reality, and we must find a way to help our sisters and brothers, whether they are right here in our home, next door, or over on the next continent. What we do for others eventually will affect us, too.

Taking the Next Steps

These psychological crises can be viewed as an indication of evolutionary progress, as humanity takes the next steps necessary for our growth. Each crisis demands effort on our part; and with each step, humanity gains a sense of freedom. When *one* of us triumphs over something that troubles *all* of us, we gain the ability to join together to end a constricting phase of duality. A recent evidence of this could be seen in Poland, when human-rights activist Lech Walesa leaped over the fence at the Gdansk shipyard to signify his solidarity with the workers. Because he took a risk by getting over the barricade, he demonstrated that he shared the suffering of the workers and that he was willing to cooperate with them to get fair treatment.

We are moving toward intelligent idealism, or into a long period of practical love and wisdom. People will eagerly discuss their understanding of the new ideals within the organism of the Hierarchy—"organism" because it is alive. At first when changes like this happen they are few and far between. Then an acceleration of consciousness will take place and the inner life of individuals will markedly shift and changes come along faster and faster. It is already happening. You may know some for whom it has happened. It may even have happened to you.

As people learn to think in terms of the whole, with concepts that include the good of other people and other forms of life, the consequences of futuristic and inclusive thinking will produce a civilization unrecognizably different from the one we now know. At present, most people talk about finances, politics, religion, and social experiences. The current basis of conversation is far removed from what people talked about 200 to 500 years ago. The subjects with which we dealt in the past several hundred years were the fodder of only advanced intellectuals and thinkers.

What does all this mean? What does it mean to you and your family? What will it mean on all levels of our lives—health, education, business, career, etc.? Regarding the future trend in the consciousness of humanity and the ways we will use our energy, one of the most significant developments will not be that we give up self-interest, but that we will be concerned about the good, the true, and the beautiful for others as well as for ourselves.

Using Our Imagination

Among the unusual qualities given to humans is the ability to use the imagination to create solutions. People can so imbue their lives with imagination, will and intention that they can act "as if," and build a psychic bridge between the soul and the personality—

or, on a more mass scale, ~~as~~ we can build a bridge that demonstrates the ability to live the higher ideals of freedom and human rights, rather than living in fear and intimidation.

The human child loves fantasy and fairy tales. Children have a powerful ability to fantasize, which helps them make choices later on in life. Good development of the imagination helps children to perceive beauty, to develop their own ideals, and to begin to develop an understanding of the subjective world. Imagination makes it possible for them to play and identify with everything imaginable. In using the imagination, children learn that they have intentionality, as well as higher values with which they can identify. The ability to think creatively also shows the way to bridge difficulties and overcome problems.

Creativity as a Primary Reason for the Existence of Human Life

Within the scope of cosmic evolution, one of the main reasons for human life is *to be creative*. Just as the beaver's whole being is constituted to build dams, so human nature seeks to work out and express creative imagination. People can use their will to bring forth their dreams and their ability to imagine not only for their own benefit, but also for others to enjoy, cooperate with, and perpetuate. The imagination and the will are so important to humankind that they constitute two outstanding qualities as proof of the divinity within us.

The long, dark, thorny, and circuitous path we all must walk now calls for all kinds of experience within us and from each one of us. The evolutionary imperative is asking us to garner the experience we will need to move from our current experience of duality to an ultimate synthesis with the divine. A single life is hardly sufficient for this task! Thus, humanity has many opportunities to develop the imagination, to lead and inspire others, and to cultivate the ability to control our physical bodies, our emotions, and the everyday mind—the chatterbox within that can unhinge emotional stability and cause havoc in our lives.

The Unseen Causes of Current Chaos

There are three major forces at work in the world today—three outbursts of energy impacting our planet at the present time—according to the teachings of the Ancient Wisdom. They are:

1. *Shamballa,* where the will of God is known;

2. The Hierarchy, or the Masters; and

3. Humanity itself.

Shamballa

Shamballa is the source of the world's most powerful energy. It is a Holy Place, known as the source where the Will of God is known—the Will expression of the One, as it works out in the everyday world that we know, in new and positive ways. It is best revealed by constructive actions. The Marshall Plan is an example of what forgiveness and the will to good can accomplish. Among its achievements have been: to rebuild and reunify Europe; to fight poverty in Africa; to assure economic growth in war-ravaged Europe after World War II; and to create policy to enable business.

Similar to the Roman god Janus, the two-faced god of Beginnings, here too, one head faces the destruction of the old—what's worn out, obsolete, undesirable, the useless and outmoded, so that new ideas, truths, and principles more consistent with the times can be expressed in the world. The other faces the energy of unification and synthesis, which ever more powerfully bonds humanity together and helps us to realize that we are one humanity, each of us but single cells in the gigantic body of humankind. It is a formidable power that synthesizes elements that have been separated and now come together for good.

The Masters (the Spiritual Hierarchy)

Another determining energy is the Masters, also called the Hierarchy, who strive constantly to let the Love of God be known. This august group of spiritually advanced beings is the center from which Love pours into the world. Their major job is to control and direct the energies that the Divine Plan is designed to materialize at this time. They watch over human and planetary events and assure that humanity moves ahead in a positive direction.

Cyclically, they make themselves known to humankind, appearing publicly to enable the divine Plan to materialize in the world.

The Christ is the Head of the Hierarchy, and works to stimulate the souls of humankind. Two thousand years ago, when He was here as Jesus, he said, "I come not to bring peace, but a sword."[1] This refers to the sword of the spirit, which the Hierarchy wields in order to end cosmic evil.

Several groups in addition to the Masters belong to the Hierarchy. There are affiliate groups that consist of initiates—those who have taken initiation; a relatively small, but growing, group. A much larger unit is made up of disciples—those who are open to new ideas and different ways of living, and who follow in the steps of the Masters, whom they view as advanced humanity. Disciples move from darkness to light, and learn to recognize and distinguish the real from the unreal. They are in the process of gaining the wisdom of soul consciousness, in contrast to an awareness of form and the world of structure (enamored of by so many people at this time).

Humanity

The final major pivotal point, as the Aquarian Age opens, is Humanity itself—one powerful moving-and-growing source of energy. Humanity is a cosmic principle, capable of expressing intelligence, a divine quality.

It is heartening to know that at the end of the 20th century, many individuals around the world understood, felt, and were conscious (at least to some extent) of the purpose of God for humanity: the expression and manifestation of love through the human race.

It may be difficult to think in terms of humanity as a *divine principle*—a principle (or qualified energy) with purpose, destiny, and meaning. Yet humanity is a fountain of intelligence. It is—we all, together, are—intelligence expressing and materializing arts, events, actions, movements, systems, and other developments that further the divine Plan on Earth. Each one of us is an embodiment of divine life—even the hardened criminal, the woman you may have just passed on the street, or members of your own family.

Shamballa, the Masters, and Humanity are closely interrelated. They are expressions of divine livingness through the human personality. When a person is receptive to the guidance of Shamballa and the Masters, first the mind, then the physical brain cells register higher impressions—just as in the movie, *Close Encounters of the Third Kind.* The major characters Roy and Gillian had an impression, for no apparent reason, of Devil's Tower in Wyoming. Roy couldn't get it out of his mind—to the extent that he actually went there, where he saw very loving extraterrestrials. Even though Roy's impression in the film was exaggerated for dramatic purposes, the point is that many of us receive impressions all the time—impressions on the brain that are so strong that they speak to us—and we are then able to express them in some meaningful way in the world. The mind enables us to receive impressions from higher levels so that we have the choice whether or not to transmit higher values and spiritual understanding.

Impressions enable us to receive and transmit higher values and spiritual understanding. The implications are astounding! They suggest that individuals can have an awareness of certain areas of divine life and consciousness that "break" the time barrier, because they have always been present and always will be. However, at present, the human physical and spiritual equipment is not yet well enough developed to receive higher information. At this point, in most people, neither the mind nor the brain are yet evolved enough to register information intended to be a phase or a step in the implementation of the Plan.

Shamballa, the Hierarchy of Masters, and Humanity are the three main centers given the responsibility—indeed, the duty—to enable, express, and execute the divine Plan. Indeed, we humans actually initiate at the level of practicality and active intelligence in the world through meditation, service, and compassion. Thus we assist the functioning of Shamballa and the Hierarchy when we learn to look behind the veil of everyday appearances and understand the good, the true, and the beautiful expressing through events, personalities, and situations that we are involved in. For example, recently, while attending a seminar on working on the Internet, as I saw the challenges and opportunities of working with it, I began to grasp a future that I had never before dreamed possible. The energy necessary for receiving this information was my openness to the new.

This great service to humanity involves understanding the qualitative energies at play in people and events. The divine qualities of truth, beauty and goodness prevail, and we can add integrity, fortitude, love, persistence, kindness, cooperation, common sense, a sense of humor, and many more qualities in people we meet every day. For example, since it was my brother's 92nd birthday, I called him to wish him a happy birthday and learned that he is planning to move into a retirement home. Here is a man who has lived fully and helped many people, who is willing to face the reality that this life cycle is nearly over. Times change and lives change. Energetically, his is a powerful choice, indicating the wisdom of acceptance—a positive state of accepting his situation, which is inescapable. Because he clearly understands what must be done, he is not wasting his or his children's time. Instead, he sees the necessity of making an open effort to do what is achievable in his situation.

You can begin to open this door in your own awareness by asking yourself questions such as: "What is happening to humankind as a whole?" "What energetic qualities are at work behind the scenes?" "How can I best serve, under the circumstances?" "What is the attitude that I choose to carry and share with others about the person, event, or situation?" "What God-like quality can I register and consciously radiate into the world, as a result of my understanding of the occurrence?" This indeed took place with frequency after the earthquake in Haiti and the tsunami in Japan.

According to the Perennial Philosophy, as people travel the spiritual path, eventually they realize that they *are* the spiritual Path. When this happens, there is no personality involvement or egotism in the recognition. The personality simply works as the One in the world, as a locus of sacred energy for the purpose of expanding Light. In a similar vein, treading the Way itself evidences a positive attitude, as people refuse to be swept away by fear, anxiety, or anger as they confront the unrest, suffering, and anguish of the time. And because they also practice silence, when they do speak, their comments are positive, compassionate, and joyful.

The Opportunity

Human life in society takes place within several monolithic areas of existence, each of which affects us in one way or another. The areas are: politics and law; finance and economics; education and learning; science and technology; religion and spirituality; psychology and self-knowledge; health and healing; work and career; relationships and family; service; ecology and the Earth; and beyond.

How are we related to these different aspects of life? To understand this, we must have a sense of what has happened to humanity in an evolutionary sense to make us the way we are at this time. Ages ago, humans were endowed with a mental faculty, which has grown and changed over a very long period of time until the human mind has become respected, educated, and creative. The mind is a hallmark of the most advanced people. Such people represent clear thinking and the best that a culture produces in its populace.

In the current passion for the desire for betterment, the principle of universality stands out as a beacon. Many people are developing and demonstrating this principle in their lives. Here are just two examples:

A man sets up a site on the Internet to be a nuclear-energy watchdog. He monitors the global political scene, and if he spots points of danger or overpowering government control, he sends out a well-worded petition to let lawmakers know the peoples' viewpoints on proposed legislation. He then sends out petitions to hundreds of thousands of people and delivers them to relevant people. The result: a shift in policy, responsibility, and behavior.

A woman close to retirement begins to fulfill her dream of developing an elder house for poor women. She looks for the right property to buy, talks to local authorities about requirements and laws, and hopes that before long she'll be able purchase a property to fulfill this dream.

It is a potent sign of human evolution, as well as a harbinger of greater justice, and more cooperation and sharing among people. It is fascinating to watch a person use this magical quality, because there is a complete (though momentary) loss of the sense of separateness. The ability to think and live with openness and expansive compassion often can be seen as an expression of universal love.

Years ago, my husband and I hosted a wonderful young Tibetan woman in our home, where she lived as part of the family for quite some time. Later, I had the great good fortune of meeting my "adopted Tibetan daughter's" own family at their home in south India. Although we had no common language and were from extremely different cultures, we got along well. The Tibetan family was utterly willing to bridge the gap. In the three or four days I was in their home, the love bond grew so strong that by the time I left, the energy of belonging was so immediate and powerful that it literally felt palpable. Distinctions and differences made no difference. There was only love, and it was far more than sentimental love (although that was present, too). Even our parting was such a rich moment that, if I could have enacted some physical posture to describe our farewells, it would have been to kneel on the ground in awe and reverence for the great tenderness showed to me by this Tibetan family. Through our "adopted daughter"— who was also their daughter and sister—each of us identified with the other. A huge opportunity had presented itself to go beyond all our known boundaries and to stretch ourselves into the infinite.

As the opening for change continues to emerge, increasingly we will see more and more people around us taking the life of the spirit seriously, and in a balanced way—free, sincere, and without fanaticism. It doesn't matter what a person's path is—whether Jewish, Roman Catholic, Buddhist, Hindu, Muslim, or some other religious or spiritual path. The important thing is that they take the spiritual life seriously and try to practice it in the best way they know, while still living a full and useful life. They demonstrate what it is to think universally and behave inclusively.

A New Phase of Cosmic Evolution

A new phase of cosmic evolution has begun, and the reason is that there are now many people all over the world who contribute and participate in massive social change, whether or not they are aware of it. These people are disarmingly close. They may belong to your City Council, live on the same street, or even be family members. They come from the ranks of common people—from a waitress to a computer programmer—and range from men to women, all classes, races, and political affiliations to the most distinguished, well-known, and sophisticated. They often have influence, and they have immense creative capacity. Perhaps one of their most outstanding qualities is their ability to tap into and use spiritual will. Sometimes this can bring about destruction—but usually, of old and obsolete forms and ways of doing things. The world and its people are tired of living under oppressive, power-hungry rulers and will no longer tolerate oppressive living conditions.

Human rights are accepted, even demanded, as necessary conditions for human life. The social change now occurring all over the world implies that humanity as a whole is sufficiently evolved to *consciously* make evolutionary adjustments. Until relatively recently, that was not the case. Now, we see more and more that the human being is the microcosm of the macrocosm. Therefore, we have a great responsibility—not only to the Earth and our environment, but also to ourselves, to each other, and to those in the animal kingdom, the plant kingdom, and the mineral kingdom. So our opportunity to evolve consciously embraces all life.

PART II

THE SPIRITUAL TREND OF HUMANITY

CHAPTER 5

HUMANITY'S SPIRITUAL DIRECTION

As our planet moves ahead and its inhabitants come closer and closer to a massive change brought on partially by the shift to the Aquarian Age, there is no turning the clock back, dislike it as some may. Ours is the call of planetary evolution: truly, a gift of the cosmos whose order and perfection have created an almost imperceptible change—that is, until fairly recently. Now, things are moving so fast that many people are dying (perhaps because the evolutionary change would be too hard to handle), or are going through extremes of difficulty as they watch the world they once knew and trusted come apart (what they look out on when they awaken in the morning is an entirely different scene than it was a few years ago), leaving little behind except destructive waste. Yet those who are wise continue to wake up with joy in their hearts.

Let's face it: all of us are in a vise. The hand of evolution is upon us! And yet the growing trend is for people to be idealistic

75

and inclusive in their thinking—a greater expression of love and wisdom in the world. This alone should give us encouragement and certainty that, despite the difficulties and challenges, we will be successful in getting through the current near-catastrophe.

The Perennial Philosophy views the movement of the cosmos and its manifestation here on Earth as fundamentally good. Behind all the problems that appear all over the world—whether massive social upheavals or difficulties of immense proportions that occur in the lives of individuals—spiritual forces and the Masters guide us as much as possible.

When reflecting on spiritual evolution, we must also consider that in the long time that humans have lived on Earth, our ancestors have moved from blind ignorance to a relatively intelligent understanding of human and planetary life. Many people all over the world—educated and uneducated, rich and poor—have assumed a greater sense of responsibility and done what they can to make life better. Clearly, the spiritual nature of women and men expands. Over the approximately 250,000 years of human evolution, the race has made great progress. Here are just a few examples:

- The fellowship and community of members of humanity has grown and expanded. We have largely grown beyond tribalism. Indeed, many people now feel themselves to be citizens of the world as well as of the country they live in.

- Humanity has moved from a condition of ignorance, in spite of rampant inequities, to healthy and concerned activities that both improve the sense of responsibility and assist those who need help.

- We have moved through the ages toward increased spiritual consciousness.

- The race has faced many huge crises of every kind, come through them, and become stronger and more intelligent as a result.

Although we still live in a world where the forces of selfishness and self-centeredness dominate, the Masters constantly work to help us shift our attitudes away from self-seeking egotism to altruistic cooperation; from the dank ravages of organized materialism to a spiritual approach to life. The Masters seek to help us learn the basic spiritual lesson is that when we cling to material possessions, we lose them; but when we give them away, they come back. They ask that we maintain an attitude of joy and remember to live spiritually.

We Are Equipped to Make the Shift

The reason we'll get through the crisis is because of the nature of humanity itself.

Our physical form is complete, after all. What's left is for us to cope with our emotions and mind. Cosmically speaking, if we as a human race direct our energies in the direction of wholeness, inclusiveness, justice, and equality for all, without exception, then as one human family we will bring on the next stage of evolution. The forces of the cosmos are with us to reveal the immediacy of higher Purpose, the presence of beauty and love, and the goodness in our brothers and sisters. And so humanity will develop a social environment that will express the fullness and glory of the inner spiritual reality. This social environment will correspond to the immense Plan at work within the cosmos, while simultaneously being in line with the greatest possibilities for the earth at this time in its history. There are groups of all sizes all over the world working in their own way to come to the aid of other people and the planet itself. This proves that there is a strong urge within the human heart to respond to major needs with integrity and solidarity. People are acting concertedly to be sources of refuge and salvation to those in need—the poor, the ignorant, the sick, the hungry, the homeless. In many cases they use technology to help. Just look at Wangari Maathai, the African woman who saw the need to plant trees in Africa and (with helpers) succeeded in planting over a million trees there. What a huge accomplishment!

The now fairly common practice of meditation all over the world sets the stage for an efflorescence of peace, caring, and cooperation around the world. The practice of meditation is probably the greatest single thing a world server can do to set things in human life aright. In meditation, seeds for a better world for all are planted.

In time we will learn the importance of silence, despite the amount of noise present from machinery, from engines, and from human speech. As we learn from the singular wisdom of the loving heart to control our speech, we will discover the true importance of speech.

We humans will discover that we have the freedom to choose whether to carry out our true purpose now, or wait until later, when we are better prepared and in alignment with our souls.

The Hierarchy of Masters is ever watchful of us. Because we have free will, they cannot and will not interfere, unless undesirable and extremely negative events occur that would prevent us from accomplishing the goal. In a very real sense, the Hierarchy is the "head center," or "pineal gland," of humanity—the will, the Plan, the essence of synthesis, the brain that makes the entire organism of humanity work. As we begin to think in terms of the *entirety* of humankind, we hasten our evolution. For among those here and alive now are people from every relevant field of endeavor, each with the necessary knowledge and experience to get us through the potential catastrophe and on to something far greater.

Illustrations from the past include Eleanor Roosevelt, who (as mentioned earlier) was the most outspoken of presidential first ladies. Not only did she raise a large family, but she also worked to aid the poor and to alert others to the importance of human rights for women. She was instrumental in helping write the Universal Declaration of Human Rights.

General George C. Marshall was influential in executing the Marshall Plan, which enabled and empowered Europe to recover and revitalize after World War II. It also paved the way to peace and plenty in Europe in the years after the war. The Plan was a constructive outworking of forgiveness. In fact, clemency is a peculiar but universally recognizable state of mind, or, in this case, a visible and tangible expression of *giving up* not only wealth by the United States, but *taking on* something—a project to rebuild other nations—that only a short time before were enemies, and importantly the mercy displayed by America was a tremendous boost to Europe.

General Marshall's plan also helped relieve some poverty in Africa. These contributions to the ongoing good of humanity have been huge. From the standpoint of the Marshall Plan's being an outpouring of love, it is notable that there was an attitude of sacrifice present as the Plan was carried out. But the ramifications of reconstruction even go beyond America's willingness to sacrifice.

The heart responded to human need and the mind formulated a plan for rebuilding war-torn countries. The focus of the energy expended during the course of the Marshall Plan's administration helped humanity gain a correct sense of proportion after World War II and enabled the embryonic development of a sense of brotherhood within humanity. As horrible as the War was, for humanity to have gained even a toehold of understanding of the principle of brotherhood was an immense and unparalleled achievement!

The Masters are the guardians and providers of our, as well as of Earth's, spiritual evolution. Spiritual aspirants, disciples, as well as those who are more advanced, want nothing more than to respond to their wishes.

CHAPTER 6

THE NATURE OF LIGHT

For ages, the human search for meaning has always conveyed itself as the investigation of light. Light has been recognized as the essence of our inner framework of existence, both in the East and the West. Enlightened beings who have come to the Earth to show us the way have brought forth light as a consequence of their realization. The Buddha is called "the Lord of Light" because he became enlightened. He attained a state of light, or illumination, because he recognized and taught the cause of suffering and the means to overcome it. Likewise, in the West, 500 years later, the Christ said, "I am the light of the world," and pointed us in the direction of the joy of service. In both cases, light was freed to sustain the world.

Our planet teems with undreamed-of life. From infinitesimally small atoms, to the Earth, to our solar system, to the great beings who guide and enable evolution, no matter how small or how large, all of this either has been or at some point will be a human. This is necessary to open women and men to the huge wave of inspiration coming from above. This aspect of evolution creates

81

receptivity to Oneness, and will enable people to communicate and build great relationships.

The story of cosmic evolution, from a metaphysical perspective, is really about the emergence of light and its increasing strength and potential in life....and *our* lives. Over the period in which humans have influenced life on earth, the light of a moral atmosphere has become evident: first as humankind's highest thought, and currently because light is emerging from humankind, even in this very moment. (We have the X-ray and Kirlian photography to prove it.) We see people manifest this light in the growing tide of goodwill around the world— as involvement in the "Green Revolution," for example, and as willing service to others in the Peace Corps, which garners the idealism and willingness to serve in its work around the world. The rise of education and the development of the discriminating and analytical faculty, enable light to pour into the world—as does the use of the Internet, which makes it possible for us to get to know and respect people all over the world.   These all are signs that humanity is now emitting physical light on the Earth.

Rudolph Steiner, the founder of Waldorf schools, taught that the spiritual nature of hierarchies is to pass through the human stage of life to become angels. As they evolve, they leave a legacy of light in the form of a moral imperative. Therefore, the kind and quality of human thought that we have, support, and nurture can enhance the quality of life not only for humans but also in other kingdoms. For example, my chickens recognize my voice when I tell them "Pet!"—they "curtsy" and allow me to caress them. The plant kingdom, too, is sensitive to human vibration, and plants can read human thoughts and emotions as easily as animals can. I once watched a scientific experiment in which a philodendron was wired to a galvanometer. When a woman expressed her gratitude to the plant for its presence there and its willingness to be part of the experiment, the pen on the galvanometer almost shot off the paper it was writing on. The plant *recognized* the woman's and the audience's appreciation!

A great deal of light is being loosed on our planet at this time. As we become increasingly aware of light, over time both inner and outer light parallels our moral development. Humans have the capability of understanding that each one of us is a unit of light— irrespective of ethnicity, country of origin, religious belief, sex, political views, race, or any other distinction—and that light is physical. However, we must understand that light appears on many different levels. It is evidence of Spirit, the presence of the soul. Kirlian photography, which has been able to document the human aura, informs us that the human physical form (among others) emits light. Very recently, scientific research has discovered the presence of bio-photons—small amounts of energy that surround the DNA in the adult human body. (There are an estimated 125 billion miles of DNA in an adult human body!) This energy informs us, just as *we* inform *it.* The quartz crystalline structure of DNA not only absorbs light but also radiates it. What this means is that it connects us to the soul and levels of being higher than the soul, just as our minds connect us to the soul. Not surprisingly, the soul is light!

Light, Morality, and Manifestation

The way humankind understands light has changed over the ages, which parallels both our growth in consciousness and in our moral development. Over a large expanse of time, the human form—including the body, the emotional field, and the analytical mind—has become more refined. We are increasingly able to receive higher thoughts and express them, especially those of universality, unity, inclusiveness, and synthesis.

The light of the soul shines brightly into the mind, finally expressing in the material world as: our developing sense of morality; our higher aesthetic sense; our ability to be empathetic and compassionate; our appreciation of art and beauty; our reflections on the Divine aspect of our nature; and our relationships with others through our developed moral character.

Behind emotion and concrete thought, which can be compared to the personality in relation to the soul, lies the realm of light. Perhaps we have always sensed this realm as an *unfamiliar* abode because we struggle with internal obstacles that seem to bar us from knowing about this beloved "far country." Trapped by our own small egos and the all-engulfing presence of the material world, we grope in the dark for a source of inspiration. Yet deep within, we know that flights and leaps are possible—through the arts, through the signals of new scientific discoveries that point to the future, and through statesmanship. When there is a will-to-good, the arts, science, and statesmanship flower. All these are the homes of light, the places where love, truth, and beauty dwell.

This book is about those divine qualities that will finally bring about a huge change on earth and in humanity—qualities that engender a greater presence of the Good, the True, and the Beautiful on Earth. These qualities increasingly manifest through science and technology, and most notably through the activity of the human heart and its expressions of compassion. People—you and I—occupy a unique place in the evolution of the cosmos. Through us, the divine life flows downward into the other kingdoms—mineral, plant, and animal—and upward to the Masters and beyond. Since humanity is a major outpost of divine Consciousness, it is a major point of force—of inspiration, goodness, and creativity. We are the microcosmic reflection of the Macrocosm.

For us, soul control is on the horizon. What a tremendous evolutionary leap! We will be able to express the nature of God—Jahweh—Ram. We will finally be able to express the mind of God, and also to be the instinctual and emotional spirit of God. What a tremendous awareness! Indeed, what an immense responsibility!

.

CHAPTER 7

THE LESSONS WE NEED TO BE LEARNING TO MOVE FORWARD

Humanity will solve the current crisis when we understand the causes for world problems and their ramifications from an energetic perspective. As evolutionary beings, we have experienced many crises in our long history as a race. The Hierarchy of Love acts on our behalf, leaving us with the hope and promise of a brighter future—as long as we learn from the very difficult lessons that currently plague us.

Human beings are the carrier of bright expectations along the time track: from very early to advanced humanity, we are ruled by divine thought through our energy bodies, that part of our being that produces the patterns our etheric bodies use to give the physical body form and substance. The etheric body is our true form, the subtle structure that is the fundamental form of the physical body. It is symmetrical and built by divine numbers, and has geometrical precision. The energy configuration within each one of us bonds us to one another, as well as to all life and all life forms. This is because we are all made of the same universal energy. We are all an integral part of the whole of creation. As we become increasingly aware of the mind and its importance, in time we can learn to bring our own minds into alignment with the Divine mind as it works and expresses through the Masters.

Unity—inclusiveness—thinking of others as well as ourselves—holding the whole in our minds and hearts—moving away from overly material concerns, and opening to our inherent spiritual aspirations and longings—coming up with new ways that will benefit the culture and planet as well as ourselves—joining groups of like-hearted and –minded people to do good— embracing our ideals, and making them work in the world. These are among the lessons we need to be learning, in order to help make the shift that humanity is needing, wanting, and in the birth-throes of right now.

Reasons for the Current Unrest

We Need a Change in Attitude about Almost Everything. Our next evolutionary steps require huge changes in attitude about everything conceivable. The evolutionary unfolding of humanity itself is a major cause for our current predicament. The things we know, and are on the verge of knowing, can be applied for selfish ends with resultant great pain—or they can be put to the service of humanity. Indeed, the intelligence within humans is so strongly awakened and vital that nothing can stop our forward movement. Our challenge is to develop a spiritual value system, especially group loyalty—that faithfulness to a group's purpose that integrates the members and works to heal disagreements with co-workers.

What needs to happen within humanity at large is already taking place individually, in many cases. Many people are starting to operate as a unified whole within themselves. In an integrated person, the personality—with its mind, emotions, and brain—works in unison. The higher octave of these forces—wisdom, love, and direction—are capable of being developed. Women and men who are intelligent, well-trained, and embody their realized integration can act as intelligent, idealistic people capable of varying degrees of leadership. Such people try to shape human thinking to a model that seems to benefit them, and their values, and to take place within the context of their knowledge and experience.

These people work in every field of human endeavor and contribute much in their area. They have an effect on civilization, and imprint their culture as well. Many have sound motives. Yet because there are those who are not experienced in the ways of the soul, they make a lot of errors. Nevertheless, the long-term effect of their actions is to stimulate public awareness, and that has many benefits for all of us.

A New Kind of Race Another reason for the current unrest is the appearance of a new kind of race. The emerging race will be distinguished by the kind of mind it exhibits. The latest race will be known for its state of consciousness rather than for its physical form. People from this racial group will be recognized for their inclusive awareness. They will have an intuitive grasp and control of many facets of energy. If this sounds far-fetched at this point, then let this description of what is to come simply open our awareness to the coming of a dimension beyond what we currently are used to. Making room for the Divine in our evolution, in itself, would change culture and civilization dramatically.

The Shift to the Aquarian Age Another major reason for the current chaos and discontent is the ending of the Piscean Era and the beginning of the Aquarian Age. Piscean principles have placed importance on authority and power, resulting in paternalism and patriarchy in the major dimensions of human life (such as family, politics, and business). The Piscean Age has been an age of male dominance, wars, and bloodshed. Keeping a "stiff upper lip" has pushed humanity to value pain and suffering. In time, as the Aquarian Age unfolds, joy will replace agony and distress.

The value of self-sacrifice will yield to the idea of sacrifice for the good of the whole. Real sacrifice is self-imposed; when sacrifice is imposed on an individual by a group or a stronger person, it amounts to coercion. We must get beyond that.

Valuing comfort and the satisfaction of every wish has led to a consumer-driven society that is doing great damage not only to the planet but also to human society. The Piscean Age has been a period of material manufacture, the rise of big business, and the emergence of the extraordinarily powerful global corporation. Advertising has told the public what will make them happy, satisfy every desire, and enable them to fulfill their dreams—all in an effort to increase profits. Old-fashioned quality of workmanship, accountability, and personal responsibility are gone. Simplicity, which should be valued, isn't. Instead, we innovate complexity and expense in every phase of our lives. The Hierarchy let this continue hoping that people would become satiated. Instead, people want more and more material goods, money, and higher profits. Men and women are not happy as a result of having a plethora of material bounty. People crave simplicity. Commercialism is still a powerful force in society, but it will not and cannot last.

Even nations are guilty, as they have committed to wars in order to possess one thing or another.

The Radically Different Nature of the Aquarian Age Another reason for disharmony is that the energies, influences, and qualities of the Aquarian Age are radically different from those of the Piscean period. The incoming forces will condition the future for approximately the next 2,300 years. Aquarius is an air sign, and air represents the mind. Alan Oken informs us that during the Aquarian time, "…universal love will be demonstrated through science, technology, education and mass dissemination of information and most of all through group, orientation and group consciousness."[1] The Hierarchy depends on the spiritual disciples in the world (not all of whom are world servers, but most of whom understand the nature and importance of service as part of their own evolution) to demonstrate the consciousness of universality and inclusiveness. These are the people to whom the global public looks to express integration and leadership in the areas of unity, synthesis, and freedom.

What We Can Look Forward To

The Internet gives us a wonderful example of what is coming in the future. There are now hundreds of thousands of websites showing that people are capable of subordinating their personalities to a greater good. There are organized groups, brotherhoods, and myriads of organizations dedicated to some phase of human or planetary betterment, or both. The amazing thing about them is that they offer an idea that members grasp, materialize, and implement for what they see as the greater good. During the Aquarian Age, we can look forward to the presence of great ideals, because humanity will have evolved a means of contact between the soul and the brain. This gives us reason for great hope! Once we are aware of the murmurings of the soul, humankind will be better able to express spiritual realities in every domain of life.

Religions will fuse into one magnificent aspiration. The presence of group life, group effort, and group harmony will be the road to spiritual values. Those practicing this new religion will call forth the mutual action of the Hierarchy.

People will find themselves drawn to one or another idealistic group, which will develop along every conceivable line of thinking and field of endeavor. Synthesis in human thinking will occur as people link together in groups and co-create ideas. The fusion of minds and effort will develop into larger and larger chains of thought, and many bridges between and among people will happen as a result. The ideas that groups will pursue and expand upon will be about human and planetary improvement.

As notable and positive outcomes, the ideals that people work on with will trace their root to the ideas of great intuitive people, otherwise known as the Masters. The ideas will filter into the streets and playgrounds of the world, where humanity will develop them—as, for example, the "Occupy Movement" is doing. As humankind works out these ideals into practical and workable approaches for the advancement of life on Earth—a remarkable mind-shift!—people will also be more open about their more spiritual yearnings and experiences. In groups, women and men will actively express attitudes of inclusiveness.

We are moving toward intelligent idealism, or into a long period of practical love and wisdom. People will eagerly discuss their understanding of the new ideals within the organism of the Hierarchy ("organism" because it is alive, creative and dynamic). At first, changes like this will happen few and far between. Then an acceleration of consciousness will take place, and the inner life of individuals will markedly shift, and changes will come along faster and faster. It is already happening. You yourself may know some for whom it has happened. It may even be you.

The current basis of conversation is far removed from what people talked about 200 to 500 years ago. At present most people talk about finances, politics, religion, and social experiences. Yet in the past several hundred years, the subjects with which we currently deal were fodder for only advanced intellectuals and thinkers. We are learning to think in terms of the whole, including concepts such as the good of other people and other forms of life. Such futuristic and inclusive thinking will produce a

ow, it
will be virtually unrecognizable.

The Message for Us

What does all this mean? What does it mean to you and your
family? What will it mean on all levels of our lives—health,
educational, business, career, etc.? The material mentioned above
clearly indicates a future trend in the consciousness of humanity,
and the ways we will use our energy. While we will not give up
self-interest, we also will be concerned about the good, the true,
and the beautiful for others.

The process of waking up is going on today all over the
world. In Paul Hawken's *Blessed Unrest,* he says that people are
more cognizant of the Golden Rule and that we are beginning to
understand the sacredness of all life.[8] The hundreds of thousands
of nonprofit organizations popping up (Hawken points out that
the numbers of groups is beyond counting) illustrate a new
phenomenon, where personal self-interest is subordinated to the
whole or to a larger group. Even though the groups work on
different problems and different facets of problems, still there is a
marked fusion and intergroup co-operation. Although working
with groups is not yet easy for individuals, the positive thing is
that it is going on constantly. These groups and their members
will make mistakes, but with time there will be fewer errors, and
people will learn to think more clearly and to recognize different
tangents of a higher truth—the forerunner of humanity's ability
to include others' truths as valid and worthwhile. What a huge
step forward!

94

Oneness and Connectedness

Humankind is constantly in the process of self-transcendence, constantly reaching beyond the borders of what we know. In our stretch afar, creativity is present. The evolution of the cosmos, as well as our own evolution, is free and open. Yet because the dynamics of the direction in which development moves and unfolds in the web of livingness, we have no other choice but to create. As individuals, we create; and so does the cosmos. We are interdependent and interconnected parts of a larger whole. As above, so below!

Creativity is little more than giving a vision some kind of form and bringing the mental image into something tangible. It is a very difficult because it must correspond to an inner experience which we cannot duplicate. It is an indication of spiritual radioactivity, and people like Leonardo da Vinci and Michelangelo were exemplars of this kind of ingenuity, as were Mozart, Beethoven, and Wangari Maathai. They undoubtedly saw vast horizons to have brought into manifestation the works they did.

Sometimes the smallest and most seemingly insignificant things can be the source of tremendous inspiration, so great that the feeling, even knowing, of interconnection and interdependence can last a lifetime. It happened to me when I was a young adult riding sitting backwards on one of Japan's famous "bullet" trains. I happened to turn my head and saw, in an instant, a young woman with a baby tied to her back carrying a lunch to her husband who has ankle deep in mud in a rice paddy. What I

95

saw lasted probably a couple of seconds, but that scene seared deep into my mind. To this day, more than fifty years later, the bright sunshine of a crisp October day lingers in my mind. The young woman, lithe as a cat, in a dark blue kimono and coat, with an infant tied to her back, quickly made her way down a hillside from the farm house. A white head dress covered her dark hair. The man in the paddy stood up straight and watched her approach with his lunch. It was an everyday occurrence for them--and to me it was fresh, new, unusual and inspiring. In that split second or two, the entire universe opened, shuddered, and reminded me that livingness is always present—and in it, the sacred is likewise there.

What the Future Has in Store

The 20th century had more wars than were fought over the previous several centuries. In the 21st century, the fighting continues. These hostilities point to a couple of significant possible results. In the first scenario, war could so exhaust humankind that all human relationships could deteriorate, allowing no hope of the human expression of truth, beauty, and goodness. In the second scenario, nations may fail to understand the realities of situations, and may neglect to come to the aid of countries fighting to develop and maintain national and individual freedoms.

It is difficult to see clearly what is going on, because humanity is engulfed in problems at all levels of the personality (some call it "the forest for the trees syndrome"), whereas the Hierarchy has the advantage of being so much more spiritually evolved that they can "see over the tops of the trees" and understand the prevailing energies affecting us in ways that we are too embedded in the personality to comprehend.

The Will-to-Good

The Will-to-Good, or creative altruism, is a huge lesson we learned in the last part of the 20th century. The world servers embody this will: more than anything, they manifest the willingness to sacrifice the small self in the interest of coming to the aid of the larger whole. Their use of the Will is spontaneous, and expresses the natural, yet unstructured, act that we often call goodwill. We recognize the will-to-good as the fundamental quality of divine purpose. It involves planned activity and a goal. Omniscience, which is eternally present, knows the Plan to achieve a higher aim. It is natural, clear about its activities, and works without effort. Imbued with cosmic love, will-to-good—at this high level—is open to new approaches, free, and creative.

The world servers are the servants of the Will-to-Good. They have worked to develop a non-separating attitude and they work constantly to build good relationships with people. They know that there is validity in various systems of government and ideologies. The door is held open as the Hierarchy looks for people, groups, and nations who live harmoniously with each other and actually live a life of goodwill.

97

"Are We at Critical Mass, Yet?"

Materialism and spirituality are powerful forces in the world. The spiritual path beckons the acceptance of freedom. Another way of life emphasizes intellectual development; and yet a third places value on possessions, the material things of life, and on aggression, which seems necessary in order to have acquisitions. Most people are still caught in materialistic values. However, as more and more people understand the worth of living on the spiritual side of the polarity, global conflicts will change.

We are the cause of the problems. Each one of us bears some responsibility for the current problems, and we each have the responsibility to create positive change. The time is here when each of us can bring in an era of goodwill, based on developing good human relations.

Are we at critical mass yet? Are there enough spiritually inclined people to overthrow the heavy weight of materialism that has dominated life for the last several hundred years? How long will we continue to support greedy and selfish regimes, to value sensory objects instead of the beauty of people, to pay astronomical amounts for military hardware and devalue life while forgetting the importance of education and human welfare? Everywhere, burgeoning out of humanity, we see creative ideas and means of solving problems. Once we turn our attention seriously to spiritual aspects of living, the world will change.

None of us alone can create an orderly change. Together, we must allow our path into the new to be illuminated by several spiritual ideas. We must meet the great, immediate needs of humanity as soon as possible, and put all our energy behind the effort. We must also remember that whatever we do must be appropriate for the peoples we try to help. Whatever we do must be the foundation for a better world in the centuries to come. The new world we build together will express the idea that all people, women and men alike, are created equal in origin and purpose, but vary considerably according to their own spiritual evolutionary development. We will come to understand that real quality leadership consists of many qualities, the most important of which are personal integrity, vision, intelligence, goodwill, and the insight that comes from trial and error.

In the coming period, people will have a well-developed sense of responsibility. This is an attitude that individuals are now developing, and in the future it will be an important part of a nation's profile. It will be understood that there is no perfect form of government or religion for all of us. No uniform regulations will be imposed, and sovereign rights of nations will be respected. There will be no "haves" and "have-nots." Even though we will go through a confusing period during the transition, we will move toward disarmament, finally realizing that wars cannot and will not solve our problems.

Quality human relations will mark the coming period. Based on justice, the recognition of inherited rights, and opportunity for everyone without exception, we will develop a high quality of education based on the awareness of the soul and its part in human life. Humanity will develop a sense of respect for divinity; a relationship to a Higher Power will be encouraged; and the spiritual Hierarchy will be openly recognized and respected. In the future, there will be more servers. Political leaders will demonstrate widespread vision. They will be selfless, and their selflessness will spread like a fire blown by the wind to more and more people.

However, before these things happen, humanity has to tackle several major problems: the racial problem, the economic problem, the problem of government, problems with religion, and the problem with corporations.

The *racial problem* will be solved as we realize that we are all brothers and sisters—that we are one, and that one blood flows through our veins.

The *economic problem* is the result of materialistic education, emphasis on competition, and the widely held idea that the weak can be used and taken advantage of by governments or greedy corporations for their profits. Humanity has to learn that by taking care of resources and using them wisely and carefully, there is enough for everyone. A better distribution system has to be created. As we approach this change, the world will need people of vision, people who have technical expertise, and people who are interested in ideas of the future and in working toward universality with kindness and through sharing and taking responsibility.

Religious problems—which have, in the past been at the root of seething tensions—will dissipate as people learn what is important about religion: the fact of oneness, the presence of love and divine Will.

The new *education* will teach the fact of our brotherhood and this will be the basis of solving many of our current problems. Corporations have too much power and far too much money. The good they could do to help the global situation has hardly been tapped.

Truly, we are at a huge crossroad, probably the most difficult and treacherous in human history. It reminds me of the time Jacob labored all night and with all his might to conquer a man who came in at night. They wrestled and wrestled, round after round all night. It was an ugly situation. And in the morning Jacob found he'd been wrestling with an angel.[3] He asked the angel for a blessing and was given the name "Israel," meaning spiritual consciousness.[4] Even though the angel won the fight, Jacob also won—for his spiritual consciousness was recognized. As long as we listen to the music that's trying to play in our hearts, so will we also win.

CHAPTER 8

IMPLEMENTING THE WILL-TO-GOOD

The planetary Hierarchy works constantly to come to the aid of humanity. Yet in this late hour, when the global crisis has reached into the remotest shadows where humans dwell, one wonders if They are working at all. Previously, and even now, They saw selfishness, self-centeredness, materialism, war-mongering, exaggerated nationalism, and a vicious tendency to act from a separatist perspective in humanity.

Will They help before it is too late? How do They assess the world situation, and view the condition of humanity as a whole, in terms of solving the current problems?

What the Hierarchy Is Seeking

The Hierarchy looks out over the sea of humanity for available human minds who will respond to the call intelligently and with kindness. How we react depends on the evolutionary process itself. Are we yet at the stage where we will no longer tolerate deception? Can we think clearly and fairly about the present situation, in all areas of life? Are human egos still so strong that, as a collective, we will sabotage ourselves by doing everything we can to destroy life on earth?

Or, are we willing to look at our behaviors and change them for the better? Is humanity finally at a developmental stage where we can truly let go of our negative emotions, which are like a metastasized cancer (that is, one begets another, and then another; all related and having a similar root, but slightly different expressions)? Are we at a stage where we can encourage productive and positive emotions to take their place? These are most difficult questions!

Because the Masters have evolved through the ranks of humanity, themselves, they know what it is like to be human. Yet because they have, since then, risen above the personal ego, the tendency to experience oneself as separate, and the negative emotions, from their elevated perspective they can see the quality and amount of light we emit and the love we give. What they look for is our ability to act in terms of the whole, and for the good of our group. What they note is how well we consider what is good for another person. What they want to know is whether we have another's welfare in mind. Their great concern is our estimation of what is good for humanity, and if we can and do think in terms of the whole. They may not be that worried about the agony or misery of people, shocking as it may seem. Just as wise parents guide their children, the Hierarchy understands the importance of discipline. Our motive is what counts. The Masters watch to see whether people are correctly oriented to the whole, themselves, and whether they live in such a way that children can learn from them so that, as adults, they can take a long, whole-centered viewpoint.

People are beginning to recognize and emulate the stronger, deeper basis of love that is an expression of the divine energy. It is called the will-to-good; and the servers of the human race respond actively and intelligently to women and men of goodwill.

Leaders and Followers of the Will-to-Good

Several groups in addition to the Masters belong to the Hierarchy. There are affiliate groups that consist of initiates— those who have taken initiation; a relatively small, but growing, group. A much larger unit is made up of disciples—those who are open to new ideas and different ways of living, and who follow in the steps of the Masters, whom they view as advanced humanity. Disciples move from darkness to light, and learn to recognize and distinguish the real from the unreal. They are in the process of gaining the wisdom of soul consciousness, in contrast with an awareness of form and the world of structure (enamored of by so many people at this time).

The Christ, the Masters, and their disciples work constantly to ameliorate hatred in the world. They do what they can to prepare for the time when the Hierarchy will externalize and be much more visible to women and men. They work hard to shield humanity from evil. This labor of love requires an immense amount of energy.

In all the crises we face, Shamballa is active. It bestows, dispenses, and disseminates the basic principle of life, the cohesive vitalizing force and the foundation of being. It consists of purpose, and is the result of the interaction between spirit and matter. It is in every form that exists within the planetary field. Its energy is vigorous and full of life. It is also the activity of the cells and atoms that make up the body—whether as a human body, an animal body, or a spiral galaxy. What this means is that spirit and energy are one and the same. This is the basis for the reunification of science and religion, which are ultimately one.

Its activity also can be viewed as the principle of destruction: it destroys in order for some new life form to arise from the obliteration, from the ashes of an outworn form.

This divine energy must express through love, or the will-to-good. (Its more natural expression is through the will-to-power; but since humanity is not ready for that, Shamballa is shifting to a stronger and deeper basis of love, which people are beginning to recognize and emulate.) The servers of the human race respond actively and intelligently to women and men of goodwill.

In addition to love, will is also a quality of Shamballa, which divides its energy in the following recognizable ways:

1. It distributes its power to disciples and initiates, who use the energy to do the building and creation that is to be a part of the next phase of evolution.

2. It fills people with the will-to-love, so that in time, hatred, injustice, and intolerance will pass. These loving people then initiate activities that lay a foundation for a better and happier human society.

The Will-to-Cooperate The will-to-cooperate within humanity will enlarge, as people come to want good relationships. People want to know—especially, given the growing presence of good education. They need to have the fundamentals of knowledge and to know the basics of both critical and creative thinking. Such knowledge will lead to wisdom.

The Will-to-Persist The will-to-persist shows up as idealism and devotion. It is a higher order of the instinct of self-preservation. Eventually, it will give humanity the impetus to believe in and also assist the Hierarchy.

The Will-to-Organize Finally, the will-to-organize will enable people to build what the Hierarchy initiates to develop a better world.

For all this to take place, both the Christ and the Buddha work at the planetary level. They labor to end wars, and to bring about those events and situations by which humanity will learn its needed lessons so we can move on and leave the crises behind. This is the way the Hierarchy works.

How You Can Help

What is left for humanity—you and me—to do? The evolutionary transformation happens one by one, as each of us does our part to make the world whole again.

Here are some ways in which you can help end the crisis:

One of the most important questions we can ask ourselves is what is my role in this change? What is my higher Self—my soul—calling me to do about the current situation? What do I have to offer? What can I do?

On the subjective side of service, we can prepare ourselves by knowing ourselves, at all levels, especially psychologically. Over time we can temper trigger points, by facing difficult emotions, looking at them, seeing where they come from and dealing with them.

In dealings with adults and children, we can try to arouse in them a sense of inquiry and interest and then suggest a direction for finding the answer, like the title of a book, a lecture being given, a television show, a story or even a movie that points out a lesson. With children particularly, we can teach them to rely on the power and wisdom of their own souls and not upon another person. We can also be willing to be a friend and share with them our deepest, highest and broadest understanding of life and its meaning. There is a great hunger in people to find others whose understanding transcends theirs!

The attitude we serve with is also important. We are told to serve with a joyous heart and with balance and even handedness. Without the joy and sincere willingness to help, the act of service means little. Real service means giving to another with a sacrificial spirit, that is, don't expect anything in return. Real service has the elements of self-forgetfulness, surrender to the needs of another, restraint, obedience to an inner calling and personal self-abandonment.

True service involves three inner qualities: integration with the person, group or situation to whom the service is rendered, alignment with your soul and the subjective cause you work with and the application of a useful method which is appropriate and useful in the situation or for the person or group involved. The act of serving is practical and is brought to a meaningful level of human experience. It can be diagrammed:

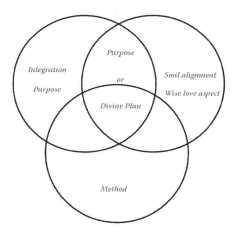

Note that the small dark area where the three circles intersect (not shown) in the center is the divine Plan, giving the activity impetus, meaning and direction and making it relate to the whole of the individual, the group, the community, and the world.

There may be as many ways to help as there are people. The ways of serving the whole are countless. Here are a few of the ways we can help to end the crisis.

Because humans have a tendency to separate and be divisive, if we are in a place or a situation where antagonism and antipathy occurs, whether at a temple, in business, at home or anyplace else, inspiring people to see the whole picture and drop their enmity is a huge service. Giving your energy to build political unity and cohesion is a tremendous service!

We are asked to live with integrity, to be honest, and to act in a way that is consistent with the highest and best that's in us. Demonstrating soul qualities is the manifestation of good character. The Hierarchy requests that we greet and celebrate the win/win achievements of the United Nations as a real expression of the Forces of Light. For instance, the Spirit of Peace can be invoked. It is an interplanetary Energy that encourages people to break through the walls of separation.

Inform yourself politically about what is going on in your own country. Participate in your nation's wholesome activities. Since the United Nations represents the whole of humankind and strives for inclusiveness and justice for all parties, it has an impact on all our lives—whether we recognize it or not!

If you are aware that the Wesak Festival (the Full Moon of May) is being celebrated, try to take part in it. During the real festival in Tibet, the Buddha and the Christ appear together for a very brief period to bless the world and bring light and love to humanity.

We all have to deal with and master our emotions. We are asked to intelligently manage the emotions by skillful use of the will and wholesome introspection. Get rid of prejudices. We are one humanity—brothers—and looking for commonalities and what we have in common can bridge gaps of unfamiliarity and difference. Likewise we are asked to refrain from criticism of other people and other nations and to think in inclusive and universal terms of the one humanity.

Those who are financially able are asked to give money to the enormous task of rescuing humanity. Large and small groups all over the world find a need and do what they can to help others just by giving their time and their hearts to alleviate human and planetary problems. In Ethiopia, for instance, medical care is very scarce. Sometimes sick and injured people have to walk or be carried hundreds of miles to get medical attention.

The Masters ask us to free ourselves of selfishness, arrogance, insular viewpoints, and self-centeredness in spite of our egos. The task is huge and demands daily conscious attention and effort.

Find some volunteer work that aligns with your interests, background, and education. If you can't find an organization, start one yourself. Many people who initiate something find in the long run that the effort brings much good to many people. The Pachamama Alliance, headquartered in San Francisco, started when the founders, Bill and Lynn Twist, went to Ecuador and found the Achuar Indians had a dream culture. In the 1980's the Achuars started to have dreams that in the near future they would be interacting with people from North America. Implausible as it seemed, it came to pass and many of the Indians have come to North America and likewise many North Americans have made trips to Achuar territory and the tropical rain forest.

One result of the interchange between the two cultures is the development of a magnificently designed symposium— *Awakening the Dreamer*—which alerts people to the seriousness of the Western approach of stewardship to our planet and suggests we need to develop a new story, a new and respectful approach, to caring for the Earth and all her inhabitants.

We are also asked to use our skills and motivation to obliterate evil, no matter how or where it manifests, whether as greed, lust for power, selfishness, tyranny, genocide, or denial of freedom. We labor for justice and security for all, and take whatever responsibility we can to aid humanity.

We often speak of the expanding universe when what we are really thinking about is the expansion of consciousness, and we are reminded that consciousness or Oneness comes about through the interrelatedness and interconnection of all living forms.

As we look at all the work there is to do on this little planet, we can find that there are definite psychological elements we must take care of like being conscious of our choices, dealing with the emotions and transmuting them as we can and moving beyond prejudice. A separative attitude does not serve anybody! There are also mental aspects of our planetary and humanity-centered serving capabilities like thinking and acting in terms of the one humanity that we can concentrate on and manifest. There are also hints from the Masters about taking on larger endeavors like working to further the work of the United Nations.

Many other suggestions can be made. What ideas do you have to help end the crisis or can you articulate a hidden dream of your own special contribution—a dream that perhaps you have harbored quietly all your life—a dream that you haven't shared—

a dream that you know you are committed to doing and being for the sake of the whole?

Each one of us has a destiny to fulfill, and your gift is special and unique to you. We have all chosen to be here at this time. Our soul's desire for life, in this turbulent time, gives us a very special possibility—and also a very difficult challenge—to discharge our duty to humanity and life on our planet as fully as possible.

PART III

HOW HUMANITY WILL PARTICIPATE IN THE COMING CHANGE

CHAPTER 9

THE PROMISE OF THE WORLD BEING BORN

Humans dislike change more than almost anything else. Yet change confronts every one of us every day of our lives, and affects every one of us all the time.

Well, hold on to your seat! The next several years will probably result in more change to our culture—even our civilization—than any previous time in human history. These evolutionary and revolutionary shifts spoken of in this book will be the scaffolding of a very different world.

A Financial System Based on Sharing

For starters, we can probably count on an entirely new financial system—hopefully, a more fair and equitable one than we have now. *Sharing* will be the dominant principle, replacing the current paradigm of competition and consumerism. To accomplish this all-inclusive change of mind, we will require a total replacement of our current values and ways of doing commerce,

117

trade, finance, medicine, manufacturing, politics, communication, and indeed all other aspects of societal life. In many ways, things will be almost diametrically opposite to the way we go about conducting our lives now.

Even our understanding of *time* will undergo an extensive change. Past and future will be merely a chimera in our minds. Only the present will have any validity.

As the Masters work more concertedly to ease us into the attitude of sharing, this change will replace the present superficial attitudes that are expected by society. While such attitudes do help us understand (by the process of acculturation) what to do in various situations, they can lead to a dead-end. As people become attached to these views, their minds close down, unable—or even refusing—to open to the practice of intelligent love and the integrity of spontaneous behavior. Instead, they grow attached to pleasantries and formalities, which then are taken to be *the* value system, *the* code of behavior. And heaven help those who stray beyond those boundaries!

All this is the ego's desire to manipulate for its own sake—a demonstration of cloying, sentimental, possessive love; a selfish attitude. And so the Hierarchy is shining a light on this, in hopes that we will be able to get beyond this and transmute it into an outlook of higher purpose and universality: genuine, creative, original, and immediately recognizable as love at its best.

However, this does not mean that instantly the world will be full of lovely, obliging people. It's not that simple. First, we all must go through many phases of growth, much more understanding of learning to love more freely and giving ourselves more completely. There will still be plenty of people who must learn to overcome greed, selfishness, and egregious self-interest.

As the principle of sharing becomes dominant in every phase of our thinking and living, as the current transformation proceeds, there is likely to be a huge financial upheaval and consequent adjustment. Before long, we'll recognize sharing as the dominant concept that motivates our lives. Business will take on an entirely new ethical standard, and its policies will be led by public opinion. It is already happening. Every day on the internet, I am asked to sign petitions, write letters to Congress, or call my Congressional representatives. In many cases, the sponsoring organizations let signers know if anything has changed as a result of signing a petition. Very often, comments and/or petitions about care of the environment, human rights, or basic policy change actually *do* force legislators to act for the people instead of for selfish interests.

Sharing is an idea whose time has come; and openness to it cannot but be a help to us psychologically.

Glimpsing the Outlines of the Emerging System

Barter We can anticipate that goods and services will be exchanged through *barter,* so that everybody benefits. National currencies, in all likelihood, will largely be a thing of the past, replaced by the barter system, along with a universal monetary exchange. Material goods and commodities will all be available through a different system. Already, communities are evolving their own currencies and some experimental alternative financial

119

systems are being tried out now. Unfortunately, since not everybody feels secure enough to participate, it is difficult to get a good reading of a particular system's success or failure, or to ascertain which aspects need to be changed to improve it.

Private Enterprise: Normalized and Controlled Even though private enterprise will continue, it will be adjusted, normalized, and controlled. Public utility companies—as well as sources of wealth such as oil, iron, steel, wheat, and rice, for example—will be owned and controlled by an international group working under the direction of national groups selected by the people and under international management.

Fair Distribution of Resources We can see the outlines of the emerging system in the background. The United Nations, as well as many governments and private organizations, have done a large amount of research and have established different agencies and methodologies. These could well be responsible for fair, equitable, and humane ways of distributing the Earth's resources so that there is a more equal "playing field."

Building a Sounder Economic System Well-educated young people will have the necessary background and analytical training to build a much more sound economic system. This will be a most difficult task, however—largely because humanity is still so mesmerized and attracted by the material world. While in the coming time the pull of materialism will be diminished, it is doubtful that it will be gone even in a hundred years. Humanity has developed the habit of turning its back on higher values, thereby willingly and gladly backing itself into a prison. Until we accept and practice higher-level spiritual values, we will continue to let ourselves be caught in the trap of materialism and all that goes with it: greed, selfishness and ego dominance.

The Principle of Sharing

According to the Perennial Philosophy, the principle of sharing governs God's purpose. This idea presides over global economics, our relationship with money, and the way we exchange goods and services. The problem is that not enough of humanity has yet discovered it.

Sharing is a quality of the soul. It enables the great work of creating relationships between people—even those we don't know. Something as basic as a pair of shoes, for instance, involves many people from all over the world. The leather may come from cattle in Argentina. Then it may be shipped to Brazil, where the leather is tanned, and made ready for the factory in Italy. After the tanned leather is shipped to Italy, Italian craftsmen make the shoes in different sizes; and again, the shoes are sent to many countries to be sold. By the time ships, trains, and trucks are considered—along with: the people who manufacture and drive the various vehicles; accountants; schedulers; middle men; advertisers; shop owners; and others who have had their part in making and getting the pair of shoes to your local shoe store— thousands of people have been involved. So the pair of shoes you end up buying involves many people—each of whom has a soul.

Humans are in control of the planet's resources. Likewise, humans have created economic problems and great suffering because of our prejudices, selfishness, and unwillingness to share.

There *is* enough to go around, once humanity develops the will to make it happen. Our perception of lack is, unfortunately, a deliberate creation, as national and corporate policies block the open distribution of goods to people who are in desperate need.

Education Is the Solution

Education is the best solution to the problem. When we truly understand deeply the place that sharing needs to have in our lives, then commodities can flow freely to those in need of basic necessities. This will counter the current practice in which the downtrodden, helpless, and vulnerable are manipulated and taken advantage of for the benefit of the greedy, self-seeking few. The misplaced values of selfishness, me-ism, personal egotism, and materialistic gain are coming to an end, or else humanity will destroy itself.

Taking a look at the entire world, we are overfeeding some, while others face starvation. Good education will teach us that there is enough to go around--if those who have plenty share with those who don't have enough. At the same time, however, there are limits to the carrying capacity of the earth. Therefore, equitable distribution of essential resources is the imperative that humanity now must master. The social systems of the past two hundred years have failed. Grounded in materialism, neither capitalism nor communism seems to work with complete effectiveness.

The Background of the Current Crisis: The Meeting of the Masters

It is said that the Masters meet every seven years. They make decisions that are related to all life forms in the world. These decisions affect the mental, emotional, and physical levels. In a larger sense, the Masters' decisions give substance to the evolutionary development of the various kingdoms in nature.

Because humanity develops though periods of crisis, the Hierarchy also has a centennial gathering at which they decide what form of crisis will prevail, what level of consciousness will be affected, and what groups it will involve, so that certain realizations and learning will result from the designed emergency. These deliberate disasters are based on past karma, and have no affect on human free will. The Hierarchy does nothing to prepare or establish circumstances that humanity must deal with.

The background of the current planetary, social, and environmental crisis started in 1925, when the Masters met. Out of this meeting, three things happened that affect us today:

1. **Release of love energy:** The first was a release of the Christ principle, or the energy of love—not sentimental love, but the love that is without emotionalism and ego-bound intent. This liberation of the power of love was felt by humanity around the world. It took, in part, the form of the growth and development of peace movements, philanthropic effort, humanitarian endeavors, human-rights recognition and goodwill. From a larger planetary perspective, the

123

spiritual goal of complete brotherhood became part of the human value system.

2. **The principle of relationship.** The second outcome of the meeting of the Masters in 1925 was the encouragement of the principle of relationship, and its effect on the myriads of relationships that humans have—to the One, to themselves, to other people, to ideas and values, to the planet, and beyond. This recognition of relatedness helped inspire people to achieve great advances in communication. The press, travel, and radio all became forces in human life. Behind this, the Masters' hidden goal was to bring humans closer to one another at the outer level so that they could develop *inner* harmony and union. The development of the Internet, and the inception and growth of global communication, is a later outgrowth of this same inspiration.

3. **Shamballa's outpouring of will and power** The third result was the outpouring of the energy of will and power from Shamballa. It is the energy of Shamballa that is behind the global crisis we all face at this time. The will of God will change our attitude to life, our value systems, and the way we perceive everything. Our current uncontrolled materialism will be replaced by spiritual and inner fundamentals of living.

Now, for the first time in human history, the great power of Shamballa impacts all of us directly. This is first time ever that Its power has not been offset and lessened in its impact. This is because so many humans have taken an initiation, or will soon do so. This gives them the creative and lovingly wise capacity to carry out the Plan. The responsibility for which humanity is now ready will help create the much-needed shift of consciousness, which is characterized by the Christ energy. We can look forward to a time of greater co-operation, goodwill, and loving understanding.

Most needed at this time of transition is the understanding that humans are spiritual beings first, and mental, emotional, and physical beings after that. This does not mean that the great work of many centuries in the fields of medicine, biochemistry, psychology, and physics, for example, was unnecessary. It does mean that people must now realize the parallel principle: a higher spiritual standard is at the forefront of all life.

The current world crisis is both about Humanity as a whole— as one single being—and about the Masters of Wisdom. When we have massive earthquakes, floods, hurricanes, and tornadoes, we see that the planet and humanity are in crisis; but only rarely do we understand what is behind it. The relationship between the Masters and humanity is being worked out through cataclysmic events, storms, earth changes, and upheavals in social institutions. The human race is an immense spiritual hub for dynamic spiritual activity, and we rarely realize this.

I hope that by now, you have started to realize this. The entire purpose behind this book is to point out that many people now

125

alive have reached an evolutionary point of highly concentrated spiritual activity. All those are responding to the tremendous spiritual stimulation of the Masters, as Humanity itself, as a whole, meets, greets, and works with the spiritually advanced beings and the energy emanating from Shamballa.

Our crisis is the result of the meeting and greeting of Shamballa, the Masters, and Humanity. This great emergency has no parallel in human history. *And yet the joyful aspect of the current, serious world situation is that if humans can meet the problems at hand, in every aspect of living, with grace and fortitude, then the entire human race will rise a notch on the evolutionary ladder to become a new kingdom.* It is similar to what occurred around 250,000 years ago, when the animal kingdom faced severe challenges and the human kingdom took shape and lived on earth. The way humankind *can* take its next evolutionary step will be the conscious unification of the Masters as a group (the Hierarchy) with intelligent Humanity.

What Really Matters: The Promise of the World Being Born

As we look at the current world predicament, with all its suffering and defeat, we see—extraordinary weather and destruction, and people so busy that they have no time to give themselves to the things in life that really matter: family, friends, sharing, helping others, and finding and using quiet time effectively, to name only a few.

Yet life on Earth will fill with promise once enough of us realize the Great Spirit (as the Native Americans call It) and build our civilization and cultural expressions on it. If we do not change, however, we can expect further social decay, deterioration of values, and lethal crystallization of traditions that no longer serve us.

Humanity is creating and stimulating the change that is occurring everywhere in the world, in every phase of our lives. Transformation abounds around us, and many things go on that are painful, unjust and cruel; and we tend to forget that we— human beings—are responsible, because of our negative thinking, addictions to pleasure and entertainment, and lack of emotional control. It is we who have evoked the death throes of our civilization.

But let's remember that death can be a good thing. A static universe where civilization never changed would be unbearable. Humanity seems to be made to develop and gradually accept new values. In some way we all participate; and as we do, we activate the death of the personality of humanity and the arrival of the soul in human consciousness.

A death of this magnitude is painful. Yet the pain purifies us, and readies us for the next step. Many are in acute distress. We suffer untold agony and fear. Many are unwilling or unable to interpret what is going on in any meaningful terms, which only increases the distress and fear. Perhaps the pain and fear rekindles the innate urge to self-preservation—which, on a higher level, is the drive toward immortality. The positive side of the present fear is

127

that it rivets humanity's attention on *life*, rather than on the lower material structures that we have held so dear.

Happily, at present humanity has a strong orientation to goodwill and altruism. People who are moving in the direction of practicing brotherhood understand and practice self-sacrifice. Their purpose, as this book has shown, is to meet the needs of groups and to build global understanding.

Will you meet the call?

THE GREAT INVOCATION

From the point of Light within the Mind of God
Let Light stream forth into the minds of men.
Let Light descend on Earth.
From the point of Love within the Heart of God
Let Love stream forth into the hearts of men.
May Christ return to Earth.
From the center where the Will of God is known
Let purpose guide the little wills of men—
The purpose which the Masters know and serve.
From the center which we call the race of men
Let the Plan of Love and Light work out.
And may it seal the door where evil dwells.
Let Light and Love and Power restore the Plan on
Earth.

ENDNOTES

The Perennial Philosophy

1. Huxley, Aldous, Introduction to the *Bhagavad-Gita*, Mentor Books published by the New American Library, 1954.

Chapter 1: Cosmic Evolution

1. Pythagoras, in "What Is a Cosmos?" *The Alexandrian*, Issue 5 (Phanes Press, Winter/Spring 1996).

Chapter 2: The Cosmic Breath: The New Story of the Cosmos

1. Jantsch, Erich, *The Self Organizing Universe;* Pergamon Press, New York, 1983, p. 300.

Chapter 3: The Impending World Catastrophe

1. Jantsch, Erich, *The Self-Organizing Universe*, Pergamon Press, New York, 1983, p 256.

2. The story is in one of the first volumes of the *Congressional Record*. It was written again by Manly Palmer Hall in his book, *The Secret Destiny of America*, from which this excerpt was taken, pp. 165–172., Philosophical Research Society. 1944.

Chapter 4: A Spiritual Reason for World Problems

1. Bailey, Alice A., *The Externalization of the Hierarchy*, Lucis Publishing Company, New York, 1989, p. 434.

Chapter 7: The Lessons We Need to Be Learning to Move Forward

1. Alan Oken, *Soul-Centered Astrology*, Bantam Books New York, 1990, pp. 232–233.

2. Paul Hawken, *Blessed Unrest*, Penguin Books, New York, 2007, p.186.

3. *Genesis*, Ch. 32: 24–32

4. *Metaphysical Bible Dictionary*, Unity School of Christianity, Unity Village, Missouri, undated, p. 304.

Chapter 8: Implementing the Will-to-Good

1. Bailey, Alice A., *The Externalization of the Hierarchy*, Lucis Publishing Company, New York, 1989, p. 434.

SNIPPETS FROM THE LIFE OF THE AUTHOR

R
ebecca A Field is a world server and founded GlobaLearn, an international educational nonprofit that was most active in India, Russia and the former Soviet Union. The organization assisted Tibetan refugees in India with business education. In Russia the group offered health and business education and taught young people how to avoid sex slavery and sex trafficking. The consequence of indentured slavery for girls and boys who get caught in this way of life is usually death.

Ukrainian work dealt with HIV/AIDS education, prevention and care.

Even though the Russian educational system has many merits and is academically superb, its graduates often lack practical business skills. Most poignantly Rebecca collaborated with a Russian nonprofit group in Saratov to bring business and health training to people in the region. She came to know about some of the boys and girls who managed to avoid the doom of sex trafficking in Russia and the former Soviet states.

Through her international work, she attended a United Nations Summit on Social Development in Copenhagen and participated in a United Nations meeting in San Jose, Costa Rica.

Originally from Denver, Colorado, she became a world traveler and now considers herself a global citizen. She resides in a small California town that has lots of pizzazz with her husband. Their two sons also live in the Golden State. The couple has a number of "heart adoptions" stemming from Rebecca's international travels. These adult children come from Tibet, Ethiopia, Russia, Ukraine, and one is an American Indian.

Rebecca has been a writer all her life. She wrote an e-book, *Wealth Creation*, to help women look at their finances in a practical and positive way. Although most of her work is academic—her latest book is alive with New Age information— *To Choose the Fire of the Cosmos*—gives hope and promise about the future of the earth and its inhabitants. The book is about humanity and its potential to be a positive force in evolution. The book lights and energizes Gandhi's statement that "We are the ones we have been waiting for."

She quips that she is part farmer and has delightedly joined the backyard chicken movement. The gratification of her life currently is her four chickens who are a constant source of entertainment and wonder. She plans to write a book about her "girls".

She holds an M.A. in Asian Philosophy, a Ph.D. in Integral Psychology, a philosophical degree with emphasis on the Perennial Philosophy, and an MHROD in Organizational Development.

Through your reading, you have created an intangible bond with the ideas contained in the book, *To Choose The Fire of the Cosmos* and with the author. If you should want to contact the writer or find what she is planning, the connecting links are below:

Email: rebecca@fieldonline.org

Website: http://rebeccaafield.com/

Blog: http://www.thecosmicfire.com

Facebook business page: www.facebook.com/TheCosmicFire

Facebook profile: www.facebook.com/rebeccaafield.

Twitter: www.twitter.com/rebeccaafield.

Linked In: http://www.linkedin.com/pub/rebecca-field/22/472/713

YouTube: http:www.youtube.com/user/rebeccaafield

Made in the USA
San Bernardino, CA
04 September 2018